Neither the author nor the publishers are res
predictions of Nostradamus, nor do the
Readers' reactions to the prophecies are
While all interpretations are offered in good
should be inferred regarding their predictive validity.

TO THE GREATEST PROPHET OF ALL TIMES
NOSTRADAMUS

De cinq cens ans plus compte l'on tiendra
Celuy qu'estoit l'ornament de son temps:
Puis à un coup grande clarté donra,
Que par ce siècle les rendra tres contens.

III:94

Five hundred years more they will take notice of him
   Who was the ornament of his times
Then of a sudden he shall give so great a revelation
   Which of that century, he will make them pleased.

On 14 December 2003, the world will celebrate the quincentenary of Nostradamus's birth. In the above quatrain he predicted that his fame will then be at its zenith, as one of his prophecies will astound the peoples of the world.

About A.D. 2003 a great decisive battle will be fought between Islam and Christianity on the banks of the River Durance in Southern France. Nostradamus has predicted that France and her allies will win the battle. This knowledge to the soldier fighting for his home and country will be the greatest morale booster he could possibly have, and France will be grateful to Nostradamus, thus enhancing his renown.

Contents

INTRODUCTION

Soon after Rome was founded, its seventh and last king, Tarquin the Proud, was asked by Sibyl, a prophetess of Cumae near Naples, if he would buy her collection of books predicting the future of Rome down through the ages. He refused to pay, saying her price was too dear. However, she was persistent. She kept returning; each time the price was the same, but the number of books was less until she brought only one book. Fearful she might not come again, he relented and paid her price. Then down through the years, the rulers of Rome, whenever a crisis arose, would consult the augurs who had custody of the book, as to what action they should take.

In the Bible we also learn that Moses brought down from Mount Sinai two stone tablets on which were engraved the Ten Commandments. Later these stones were placed in a specially-made gold-plated casket named the Ark of the Covenant, kept first in a Tabernacle then in the Holy of Holies in Solomon's Temple.

Again when the Hebrew Judges and Kings were in a quandary they would request their high priest to consult the Ark of the Covenant for its advice. During the years when Israel took its advice, the country prospered. After the Ark of the Covenant mysteriously disappeared in about the 6th century B.C., the Hebrew's fortunes progressively deteriorated until they became nomads without a home. It is only in this century that Israel has again found a country of its own.

France has been most fortunate. For almost 500 years she has had a prophet of her own and, like Rome's Sibyl, has had bequeathed to her a book called the Centuries in which the author foretold France's vicissitudes accurately for the past 500 years and onto the year 3997. His name was Michel de Nostredame, better known in its Latin form as Nostradamus.

We common mortals today are more privileged by being able to buy a copy of the Centuries in any good bookstore. In past generations, only learned scholars had access to a copy. Since 1781 it has been on the banned list for those of the Roman Catholic faith.

> The lady furious, enraged at the adultery
>   Shall come to her prince to conjure him to say nothing.
> But soon, the abuse becoming known,
>   It will make the seventeen seem martyrs.
>
> [VI:59]

To Nostradamus interpreters this apparently innocuous account of scandal in a minor principality was of little importance. But recently, the heir apparent to the British monarchy, Charles, Prince of Wales, has publicly admitted the adultery predicted, thus throwing the whole future of the British monarchy into jeopardy – the meaning of the last line. The 'seventeen' are the Queen and the immediate members of the royal family who are unable to intervene and so are innocent victims or 'martyrs' of the whole affair.

However, let us look at the origin of this remarkable man, whose predictions are as interesting today as they were in his lifetime.

Michel De Nostradame was born on 14 December 1502 in St Remy in Provence, then independent but now part of France, of Jewish parents – the first of five brothers. Little is known of the brothers except that the youngest, Jean, wrote ribald songs and commentaries and later became Procureur of the Parliament of Provence. When Nostradamus was nine, his family, under religious pressure, became Roman Catholics. That he was a sincere one can be shown by his prejudice against other beliefs in his predictions.

Nostradamus displayed early intelligence at an early age, so his grandfather, Jean, began to teach him Latin, Greek, Hebrew, mathematics, and what was then termed 'Celestial Science' or astrology.

He then went on to Avignon, a former Papal seat and the repository of a famous library. His keen interest in astrology soon became known among his fellow students. Also he believed, like Copernicus, that the world was a sphere and was rotating around the sun. Nostradamus believed this a hundred years before Galileo proved this by telescope.

When he turned eighteen, Nostradamus was sent to Montpellier to study medicine. Three years later he received his Bachelor's Degree, thus allowing him to practise. In XVI century Europe, very virulent plagues were prevalent and doctors were few, especially those willing to risk their lives treating the poor. As he went around the countryside dispensing his own medicines, Nostradamus's fame grew rapidly. Then, after having travelled extensively throughout south-western France, he returned to Avignon to further his studies. Among his patients now were some very important people and his handsome fees allowed him to publish a book about his cures and ideas on medicine. In 1529, now aged 26, he returned to Montpellier to study for his Doctor's degree.

On receiving it, he continued as a teacher, but his nonconformist ideas, and his refusal to bleed his patients (in an era which believed one's sins were the cause of one's disease and so had to be bled out of the system) caused disfavour with the faculty. He left, and once again took to the road until in the city of Agen, he was invited to call upon Julius César Scaliger, second only to Erasmus for having the finest intellect of the age.

Scaliger became his patron, so Nostradamus settled in Agen and married a girl of 'high estate, very beautiful, and admirable'. Her name has not been recorded, but we know they had two children, a boy and a girl. All was going well for Nostradamus – a good patron, a happy marriage and a thriving practice – when a series of misfortunes hit him. A plague struck Agen, which, despite all his efforts, wiped out both his family and his practice. A dispute with Scaliger ended his patronage; then his wife's family demanded the return of her dowry. Finally, Nostradamus was sent for by the Church to defend himself against an accusation that, some years before, he had made a blasphemous remark. So, discretion being the better part of valour, he once again took to the road. For six years he travelled throughout Lorraine, then to Venice, then down as far as

Sicily, visiting the apothecaries in every city, comparing their treatments with his own. Apparently his deep sorrow at this time brought on his prophetic abilities.

While travelling in Italy, Nostradamus met a group of monks. Going up to a young acolyte, he asked for a blessing. The older monks reproached him and asked why he had not requested one of them to perform the ritual. Nostradamus replied, 'I must always be blessed by His Holiness.' Nineteen years after Nostradamus's death, the acolyte, Felice Peretti, became Pope Sixtus V.

An amusing story is also told of this time. A nobleman, Seigneur de Florinville, invited Nostradamus to dine with him, but first asked Nostradamus to see his farmyard. He then pointed out two piglets, one black and the other white, and asked Nostradamus which of them they would dine on that night. The reply was, 'The white.' De Florinville secretly told his cook to kill the black one. After the meal was over, the host boasted to his guest that they had eaten the black piglet instead of the white, as he had predicted. Nostradamus answered, 'No, we ate the white.' Triumphantly, the Seigneur called the cook to prove his guest wrong. But the cook, when confronted with Nostradamus, confessed that he had laid the black piglet ready for roasting before a window, but a wolf had leapt in and carried it off. So he had been forced to kill the white piglet to provide the meal.

In 1554, Nostradamus settled in Marseilles at a time when Provence suffered one of its worst floods in history, and a plague was rampant. Rotting corpses floated through the countryside and doctors fled. Aix, the capital, was so desperate that it called on Nostradamus for help. He went there and, working alone, introduced hygienic measures. Insisting on clean water and fresh air, he eventually brought the pestilence under control. Soon a call came from the city of Lyons, which was also stricken with the plague. The grateful citizens of both cities rewarded him handsomely for his services, which he in turn shared with the poor. He settled in Salon, where he married a rich widow, Anne Ponsart Gemelle. The fine house where they lived still exists today and is open to visitors. The upper floor of the house was converted by Nostradamus into his study. Here in the late hours of the night he would, whilst meditating, have his visions and write them down in his books.

Some, he claimed, he burnt – no doubt a ploy to deceive the spies of the dreaded Inquisition.

A former mayor of Beaune, Jean de Chavigny, became Nostradamus's pupil in astrology and astronomy and later wrote several tracts about his master, besides assisting in editing his papers after his death. Certainly he was the editor and interpreter of the first compilation of Nostradamus's *True Prophecies or Prognostications*. The first (1555) edition consisted of only six and a half centuries, containing predictions from then until the end of the world. The complete edition with the missing centuries was published in 1568, two years after his death.

The centuries, incidentally, do not mean years but are chapters, each of 100 quatrains, or four-line rhymed verses. They are all jumbled up as regards timing and relationship; also, the words are a mixture of local Provençal, Greek, Latin and French, interlaced with meanings taken from ancient Roman and Greek mythology. Sometimes he coined his own words to suit the verse's needs as to rhyme. He commonly used anagrams and words such as 'Hister' for Hitler. There were reasons for this, of course, one of them being the danger of being burnt at the stake if condemned by the Church or the Inquisition as an instrument of the Devil. Also, being a scholar and thus one of the elite of this world, he did not wish his work to be misconstrued by fools or ignoramuses. The following quatrain he left as a curse to such people:

THOSE WHO READ THESE VERSES, LET THEM
   CONSIDER WITH MATURE MINDS,
LET NOT THE PROFANE, VULGAR AND IGNORANT
   BE ATTRACTED TO THEIR STUDY.
ALL ASTROLOGERS, FOOLS AND BARBARIANS DRAW
   NOT NEAR,
HE WHO ACTS OTHERWISE, IS CURSED
   ACCORDING TO RITE.

Right from the start, the Prophecies had an astonishing success. Overnight, Nostradamus became famous throughout all France and Europe at a time when books were expensive and the majority of people illiterate. The King and Queen of France soon sent for

Nostradamus. The Queen, Catherine de' Medici, arranged for a coach, and for horses to be positioned in stages all the way to Paris, to which he arrived in four days instead of the normal eight. On arrival, he booked a room in an inn close to Notre Dame cathedral, but was immediately granted an audience with their majesties. The Queen's audience with him lasted several hours but the King was not so impressed, staying barely a few minutes. The royal couple gave Nostradamus 130 gold crowns, despite the fact that the journey had cost him 100. However, they did him the honour of having him lodged with the Archbishop of Sens in his palace for a fortnight. While there, many notables flocked to see him and he prepared horoscopes for them and made out predictions.

The Queen sent for him again to chart the futures of all the family members despite the fact that he had already predicted some of their fates in his recent book. However, he told her that among her sons there would be four kings. The eldest, Francis II, reigned only just over a year before dying. The future Henry III was King of Poland before resigning to become King of France.

Word came to Nostradamus that the Justices of Paris were inquiring into his magical practices, so discreetly he decided to return home. On his return he found he was now a man of some renown, but he began to suffer from gout or arthritis, so he devoted his time to eminent visitors and completing his Prophecies. Two predictions up to that time to have come true were of the King's death (I:35) and that of his son, Francis II (X:35). Even with such a powerful patron as the Queen, these were dangerous events to have happened.

In 1564, the Queen and her second son, Charles IX, and their court decided to make a Royal Progress throughout France. Over 800 composed the royal party and the tour took two years. Naturally when it reached Salon, it stopped to see Nostradamus. The Queen stayed at his home for two days, receiving his advice while she admired his family. On her departure, she gave him 300 gold crowns and made him Physician-in-Ordinary to the king, an office that carried a stipend and some fringe benefits, no doubt very pleasing to the old prophet.

A very human incident occurred while the royal party was at Salon. When Nostradamus saw some moles on a small boy, a member of the party, he wished to examine them, but the boy was shy and ran away. Moles on the body were a popular form of divination at that time.

On inspecting the moles when the boy was asleep, Nostradamus declared that one day the boy would become King of France, which he did later, becoming king as Henry IV, one of France's most revered monarchs.

The crowning moment of his life having passed, and his gout having developed into dropsy, on 17 June 1566 he made his will, and died a fortnight later. He left the then enormous sum of 3,444 gold crowns. He was interred upright in the walls of Salon's Church of the Cordeliers, in which his wife erected a grand marble plaque to his memory. During the French Revolution, roving soldiers, expecting to find loot, opened the tomb but fled when they read the message they found inside. Later his remains were reinterred in the Church of St Laurent, where they remain to this day.

When the Revolutionary mob stormed the Bastille in 1789, they found a copy of the Centuries opened at a page foretelling exactly what they had just been doing. Later on, Josephine is reported to have drawn Napoleon's attention to the many quatrains Nostradamus wrote about him, just as Dr Goebbels's wife made Hitler aware of the 'Hister' verses.

Since Nostradamus's death many reissues of the Prophecies have been made, sometimes up to 30 a decade, not counting many spurious ones. In those days, copyright laws did not exist, so plagiarism was rampant. Both the Church and state frowned on prophecy, recognising only those of Holy Writ. In 1572, 20 booksellers were fined for selling the Prophecies. Predictions were frowned upon, and their fulfillment seen as curses incurred by their authors. After the Great Fire of London, a committee inquired into Nostradamus because he prophesied it. Nowhere did he contradict Biblical prophecy, yet in 1781 the Vatican's Congregation of the Index banned the Centuries from being read by the faithful.

Since Nostradamus was a Frenchman by adoption, he wrote the Centuries with a French bias and most concern France. As for Great Britain (which he called 'the Isles' or 'Great Neptune'), a country closely associated with the destiny of France, it has the next most frequent mention; then Europe as a whole and, finally, the rest of the world.

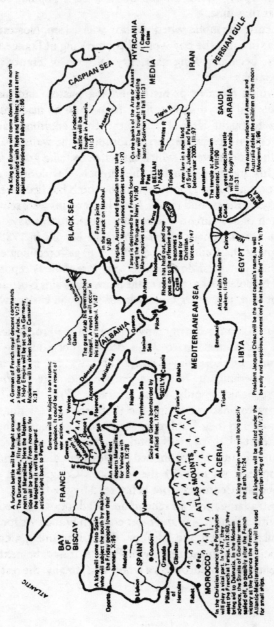

The Christian Advance and the Moslem Retreat Back to the Caspian Sea

THE PROPHECIES OF NOSTRADAMUS IN HISTORICAL ORDER

1

FRENCH HISTORY

The reigning monarch in France when the Centuries was first published was Henry II, a most able statesman married to an equally able woman, Catherine de' Medici. They had seven children, three of whom were to follow their father on the throne. France at this time was under the feudal system, the King being merely an overlord. The country was divided into duchies, any of which was likely to challenge the King for his throne. It was also a time of religious strife, simmering close to civil war between the Protestants and Roman Catholics. So a state of chaos varied from king to king depending on his ability. Advised by Cardinal Richelieu, it took the long reign of Louis XIII to consolidate the monarchy.

Here is a list of kings from Nostradamus's day to the end of the monarchy.

Monarch	Reigned
Henry II	1547–1559
Francis II	1559–1560
Henry III	1560–1589
Henry IV of Navarre	1589–1610
Louis XIII	1610–1643
Louis XIV	1643–1715
Louis XV	1715–1774
Louis XVI	1774–1792

Louis XVII, the Dauphin	1792–1793
The Revolution	1793–1804
Napoleon I	1804–1815
Louis XVIII	1815–1824
Charles X	1824–1830
Louis-Philippe	1830–1848
Second Republic	1848–1852
Napoleon III	1852–1871

France will see many changes – from kingdom to empire.

> *Regne Gaulois tu sera bien changé*
> *En lieu estrange est translaté Empire*
> *En autres moeurs et loix seras rangé*
> *Rouen et Chartres te feront bien du pire.*
>
> III:49

Realm of France, you will see great change;
  Of a strange place you'll alter to an Empire.
In other manners and laws you'll range,
  Rouen and Chartres will do you harm.

A remarkable prophecy of changes France was to undergo, changing colonies into an empire; changing from a monarchy to a republic; and the adoption of the Napoleonic code. The harm mentioned in the last line may be yet to come.

Henry II annoyed to see ill-treated children taken prisoner.

> *Freres et soeurs en pluieurs lieux captifs*
> *Se trouveront passer pres du monarque*
> *Les contempler ses rameaux ententifs*
> *Desplaisant voir menton front nez les marques.*
>
> II:20

4

Brothers and sisters captives from various places,
    They shall pass before the monarch.
Who shall look upon them with sad eyes
    Displeased to see their chins, foreheads and noses.

An episode in Henry II's reign when, to his displeasure, children captured in a civil war were paraded before the King after being treated like animals.

Henry II mortally wounded in a jousting duel.

Le lion jeune le vieux surmontera
    En champ bellique par singulier duelle,
Dans caige d'or les yeux lui crevera
    Deux classes une, puis mourir mort cruelle.

I:35

The young lion shall overcome the old
    On a martial field in a single duel,
In the golden cage his eye shall be put out,
    Two wounds in one; then he shall die a cruel death.

This is Nostradamus's most famous prophecy, which proved true only four years after the publication of the Centuries. In an age when knights-in-armour still dominated the battlefield, Henry was proud of his courage and skill in the art. He held a tournament in honour of the double wedding of his sister Elizabeth to Philip II, King of Spain, and his daughter Marguerite to the Duke of Savoy. The King entered the lists against Count Montgomery, the captain of his Scottish guard. After two unsuccessful bouts the King insisted on a third. Reluctantly the Count took up the challenge. Both men were wearing golden coloured helmets. The count's wooden lance shattered and a splinter entered the King's helmet, mortally injuring his eye, the wound causing him to die a painful death 11 days later.

The French Court in dismay as Henry II lays dying.

En l'an qu'un oeil en France regnera,
  La Court sera à un bien facheux trouble;
Le grand de Blois son ami tuera
  Le regne mis en mal et doubte double.

III:55

In the year, the one-eyed shall reign in France,
  The Court will be in very great trouble;
The great one of Blois will kill his friend,
  The realm will be bad and in double doubt.

The one-eyed was the dying Henry II, who lingered on for 11 days.
The queen was inexperienced in affairs of the state and the new king
only 17 years of age, the other children even younger. A brother was
later to have two cousins murdered, hence the third line.
  The last line refers to the two religious factions that were now to
sap the energies of the kingdom.

Henry II's widow has Count Montgomery abducted in his bed.

Celui qu'en luitte et fer au fait bellique
  Aura porté plus grand que lui le prix,
De nuict au lict six lui feront le pique,
  Nud sans harnois subit sera surprins.

III:30

He who in a struggle with weapons in a martial deed
  Shall carry off the prize from a greater
By night six shall harm him in his bed,
  Nude without weapons, he shall be suddenly surprised.

Queen Catherine de' Medici, despite her husband's pardon, never
forgave Count Montgomery's part in her husband's death. On her
orders the Count was seized in his bed at night and lodged in the
Conciergerie, or state prison.

St Quentin taken by the Spaniards in a surprise attack in 1557.

Pres de Quintin dans la forest Bourlis,
  Dans l'Abbaye seront Flamens tranches,
Les deux puisnais de coups mi estourdis
  Suitte oppressee et garde tous aches.

IX:40

Near St Quentin in the Forest of Bourlis
  In the Abbey the Flemish will be slashed,
The two youngest, half-stunned and crushed,
  Followers crushed and guards cut to pieces.

This quatrain warns of a surprise attack that took place in 1557. The previous day the Spanish had taken the Abbey of Vermandais, then the action as described took place.

Henry II retired his famous admiral, who then led the Huguenots.

Le grand pilot sera par roy mandé,
  Laisser la classe pour plus haut lieu attaindre,
Sept ans apres sera contrebandé
  Barbare armee viendra Venise craindre.

VI:75

The great Pilot will be by the King ordered
  To leave the fleet, for a higher attainment
Seven years later, he will be in revolt.
  The Barbarian army will come to make Venice afraid.

Admiral Gaspard de Coligny was Henry II's admiral of the fleet. When he was retired in 1559, he then became leader of the Huguenots or Protestant party. As such, he became in opposition to the next King, Charles IX. The last line is another prophecy altogether: a Turkish assault on the Venetian-held island of Cyprus.

7

The infamous massacre of St Bartholomew's Day, 1572.

Le noir farouche quand aura essayé
  Sa main sanguine par feu, fer, arcs tondus;
Trestout le peuple sera tant effrayé
  Voir les grands par col et pieds pendus.

IV:47

The ferocious King when he has tried
  His bloody hand by fire, sword, and bended bow
All the people will be so afraid
  To see the nobles hanging by their neck and feet.

'Noir' is an anagram for 'roi'; king. This quatrain foretells the dreadful nationwide massacre ordered by the boy-king Charles IX. The last line describes the fate of Admiral De Coligny, whose body was hung by his feet from a gibbet and displayed in a Paris square.

The dowager Catherine mourned for seven years and was then regent for many more.

La Dame seule au regne demeuree
  L'unique estaint premier lict d'honneur,
Sept ans sera de douleur exploree
  Puis longue vie au regne par grand heur.

VI:63

The Lady shall be left to reign alone
  The unique one first dead on the bed of honour
For seven years she will weep with grief,
  Then a long life to reign for a great time.

After Henry's death, and since the next two kings were minors, Queen Catherine de' Medici ruled as Regent for many years, the meaning of the first and last lines. This verse has often been applied to Queen Victoria and her Consort, Albert, but I believe this is the correct place for this verse.

Queen Mother furious to learn Henry III has had his cousins murdered.

Par la response de Dame Roi troublé,
Ambassadeurs mespriseront leur vie,
Les grand ses freres contrefera doublé
Par deux mourront ire, haine, ennui.

I:85

The reply of the Lady shall trouble the King,
The ambassadors shall fear for their lives,
The greater of the brothers will disguise the action
For the two will die by ire, hatred and envy.

Catherine de' Medici was furious when Henry III had his two cousins, the Duke de Guise and his Cardinal brother, murdered. The Ambassadors were the Estates to whom the King tried to explain his actions. 'The greater' was the Duke of Mayence, who escaped death.

Mary Queen of Scots' husband, Francis II, childless, dies young.

Premier fils, veufve, mal'heureux marriage,
Sans nuls enfans, deux isles en discorde,
Avant dixhuict incompentant aage,
De l'autre pres plus sera l'accord.

X:39

First son, a widow, an unhappy marriage
Without children, two isles in discord
Before eighteen, an immature age;
Of the other, even less the accord.

Henry II's eldest son, Francis II, was married to Mary, Queen of Scots. A sickly lad, he died barely 18, leaving no children. 'Two isles in discord' warns of the strife she was to cause in Britain on her return there. The last line refers to the next King, Charles IX who was only 11 when he married.

Mary, Queen of Scots quarrels with her mother-in-law.

Les malheureuses nopces celebreront
En grand joye mais fin malheureuse
Mary et Mere Nore desdaigneront
Le Phybe mort et Nore plus piteuse.
X:55

The unhappy marriage will be celebrated
With great joy, but the end will be unhappy.
Mary and Mother-in-law will quarrel
The Phybe dead, daughter-in-law pitiful.

Mary, Queen of Scots was a king's daughter and as her mother-in-law was a 'merchant's daughter' she considered herself the superior. 'The Phybe' would be her father-in-law, Henry II.

France totters between peace and war: a policy is lacking.

La paix s'approche d'un costé, et la guerre
Oncques ne feut la poursuitte si grande
Plaindre homme, femme, sang innocent par terre
Et ce fera de France à toute bande.
IX:52

Peace nears on the one side, the war
On the other, never a pursuit so great.
Piteous men, women, innocent blood on the ground
And it will be in France all around.

In 1559 the King of France made peace with Spain, to concentrate on religious matters that were dividing the country. With three kings in two years, policy and direction were lacking.

Henry III plans murders in Paris but they take place in Blois.

Paris conjure un grand meutre commetre,
  Blois le fera sortir en plain effect;
Ceux d'Orleans voudront leur chef remettre,
  Angers, Troye, Langres leur feront un meffait.
  III:51

Paris will conspire to commit a great murder
  Blois will cause it to be carried out.
Those of Orleans will want their chief restored
  Angiers, Troyes, Langres will do them harm.

Henry III planned the murders in Paris but the Duke de Guise and his brother, a Cardinal, fled to Blois where they were murdered by the king's bodyguard. Orleans at this time revolted.

Pope Sixtus V is afraid to punish Henry II for his misdeeds.

Quand chef Perouse n'osera sa tunique
  Sens au couvert tout nud s'exposlier,
Seront prins sept faict aristocratique
  Le pere et fils morts par points au collier.
  V:67

When the chief of Perugia dare not risk his tunic
  Without cover and expose himself nude,
There will be seven taken for setting up an aristocracy
  Father and son will die by points in the collar.

The chief of Perugia was the Pope, Sixtus V, who had excommunicated Henry of Navarre, so he could hardly do the same to Henry III

11

without losing badly needed revenues from France. Already he had lost those of England and the Northern countries. Henry III and his father, Henry II, both died from pointed weapons, not in the neck, but in the stomach and in the eye.

Henry III stabbed to death at a council meeting.

Ce que fer, flamme n'a sceu paracheuer,
La douce langue au conseil viendra faire
Par repos, songe, le Roy fera resuer,
Plus l'ennemy en feu, sang militaire.

I:97

What neither iron nor flames could do
Shall be done in a council by a sweet tongue
Asleep, in a dream, the King will think
More the enemy in fire and martial blood.

Henry III called on Henry of Navarre for assistance. A Council was held, during which a monk named Clement claimed he had a secret message. As the King bent low to hear, the monk plunged a dagger into the royal stomach. Some time previously, the King had had a dream in which the emblems of Royalty were being trodden upon by the clergy and the rabble, which is the meaning of the last two lines.

Fear of the Spaniards will cause Henry of Navarre to raise the siege of Paris.

Amour alegre non loing pose le siege
Au Sainte Barbar seront les garnisons,
Ursins Hadrie pour Gaulois feront plaige,
Pour peur rendus l'armee aux Grisons.

X:38

Cheerful love will not hold the siege for long
    At St Barbar will be the garrisons
Ursini, Hadrie for the French will give pledges
    For fear the army given to the Grisons.

After Henry II's death, Henry of Navarre continued to besiege Paris but the advancing Spanish armies from the north caused him to raise it. 'Cheerful Love' was a term used by the French for Henry just as 'Hadrie' was a pet name used by Nostradamus for him. To unite the French and also to gain the throne, Henry changed his religion ('Paris was worth a mass') and also to avoid his troops deserting to the Grisons, Spanish mercenary troops. The Ursini, or Orsini, were Papal friends of Henry.

When the contender murders his guests, Henry of Navarre is made King.

Dans le conflict le grand qui peu valloit.
    A son dernier fera cas merveilleux
Pendant qu'Hadrie verra ce qu'il falloit
    Dans le banquet pongnale l'orgueilleux.
                  II:55

In the conflict the great one of little value
    At his last try will do a marvellous thing,
While Hadrie will do what is needed,
    During the banquet the proud one will be stabbed.

The 'great one' and the 'proud one' was the Duke of Mayence, who invited the members of Parliament to a banquet and then had them treacherously murdered. Henry of Navarre at once changed his religion and was accepted as King of France.

High will be low and low will be high when the House of Vendome rules in Paris.

> Le ranc Lorrain fers place à Vendosme,
>   Le haut mis bas et bas mis en haut,
> Le fils d'Haman sera esleu dans Rome,
>   Et les deux grands seront mis en defaut.
>
> X:18

The House of Lorraine will give way to Vendome,
    The high pulled down, the low raised up.
The sons of Haman will be elected in Rome
    And the two great ones will lose.

Navarre was a small principality created as a buffer zone between France and Spain. Its ruler, Henry, had married a daughter of Henry II of France and now, since all her brothers were dead, she had a claim to the throne. Henry was poverty stricken, with few resources compared to his rich neighbours. Now he was King of France, the 'low' had been raised up. Henry was to Rome a heretic, but now, as a King, he had to be recognised in Rome, the meaning of the third line.

The Great King Henry IV ruled wisely and well.

> Le prince rare en pitié et clemence
>   Apres avoir le paix aux siens baillé,
> Viendra changer par mort grand cognoissance
>   Par grand repos le regne travaillé.
>
> VII:17

The prince, rare in pity and clemency,
    After he has given peace to his subjects
Shall come after death to change knowledge
    Out of the great rest the realm will be troubled.

Under Henry II of Navarre, as Henry IV, France had an enlightened monarch. His Edict of Nantes gave his subjects religious freedom and his peace allowed progress to be made. The last two lines mean his worth was not appreciated until after his death.

After a 21-year reign, Henry of Navarre is assassinated.

Les armes battre au ciel longue saison,
  L'arbre au milieu de la cité tombe,
Verbine rongue, glaive en face Tison.
  Lors le monarque d'Hadrie succombe.
                                III:11

The arms will battle in the sky for a long season,
  The 'Tree' shall fall in the city centre.
The sacred branch cut, the knife opposite Tison,
  Then the monarch, Hadrie succumbs.

Throughout his reign religious strife was ever present. The 'tree' that fell and the 'sacred branch' that was cut, was 'Hadrie', Nostradamus's pet name for Henry of Navarre. The king was assassinated, stabbed by a maniac named Ravaillas in the Rue Feronnierre, opposite the Rue Tison in the centre of Paris.

Concini, Marshal D'Ancre, hanged for stealing public funds.

L'arc du thresor par Achilles decu,
  Aux procees sceu la quadrangulaire
Au faict Royal le comment sera sceu,
  Corps veu pendu au veu du populaire.
                                VII:1

The Arc of treasure deceived by Achilles,
  Shall show to posterity the quadrangle,
By the Royal deed the comment will be known,
  The corpse seen hung in public sight.

The demise of Henry IV left Louis XIII to reign as a minor. Henry's second wife Marie de' Medici, became Queen Regent. She left favourites to govern with a free hand. An Italian, Concini, Marshal d'Ancre, exploited his position to the utmost. But he was exposed by Achilles de Harlay, the President of Paris, and the king ordered his execution in the Quadrangle in front of the Royal Palace. Later his body was hung from a gibbet for public exhibition.

The boy-king seizes power from his mother.

L'enfant Royal contemnera la mere
Oeil, pieds blessés, rude inobeisant,
Nouvelle à dame estrange et bien amere,
Seront tués des siens plus de cinq cens.
VII:11

The royal infant shall despise his mother,
Eye, feet wounded, rude, disobedient,
New to a lady, strange and so bitter,
There will be slain about five hundred.

Advised by his counsellor, Cardinal Richelieu, Louis XIII seized power from the Queen-Regent. In the ensuing action with the Queen's Guard some five hundred were killed. The queen went into exile, never to return.

Louis as the Dauphin, the first to carry the Lily of France.

Le Lys Dauffois portera dans Nancy,
Jusques en Flandres electeur de l'empire,
Neufue obturee au grand Montmorency,
Hors lieux prouvez delivre à clerepeyne.
IX:18

The Lily of the Dauphin will be carried into Nancy
As far as Flanders, the Elector of the Empire.

New obstacle for the great Montmorency
Out of approved places delivered up to Clerepeyne.

As the Dauphin, Louis XIII was the first one to carry the Lily as the emblem of France when he took Nancy and freed the Elector of Treves from Spanish captivity. About the same time, 1632, a revolt was led by the Great Montmorency which failed, and he was taken prisoner. He had plotted with the king's brother and, being popular, all Europe pleaded for his life. But the Cardinal advised the King to make an example of him to consolidate the royal authority. He was transferred to the newly built Hôtel de Ville. As a concession, he had a private executioner instead of a military one. 'Deliver Clerepeyne' has two meanings: 'deliver to clear punishment' and 'Clerepeyne' was the executioner's name.

The traitor Prince Louis de Condé slain after the Battle of Jarnac.

Bossu sera esleu par le conseil
  Plus hideux monstre en terre n'apperceu,
Le coup voulant crevera l'oeil,
  Le traitre au Roi pour fidelle reçu.
                                    III:41

The hunchback will be elected by the council,
  A more hideous monster has never appeared on Earth,
A flying shot shall pierce the eye.
  A traitor to the king who received his fidelity.

Prince Louis de Condé, a hunchback, was a Huguenot leader who had several times sworn his allegiance to Louis XIII. Upon his surrender after the Battle of Jarnac, 1569, he was deliberately shot down by an arrow.

Louis XIII's adviser, Cardinal Richelieu, will be avaricious.

Prelat avare d'ambition trompé
Rien ne sera que trop viendra cuider
Ses messagiers, et lui bien attrapé,
Tout au rebours voir, qui le bois fendroit.

VI:93

The greedy prelate deceived by ambition,
  Shall do nothing but covet too much,
He and his messengers well trapped
  When they see one cut the wood wrong way.

This quatrain foretold the failings of Cardinal Richelieu, whose greed had no limits. His accumulated wealth enabled his relatives to marry into the nobility of the land.

Cardinal Richelieu replaced by Cinq Mars who betrays his king.

Vieux Cardinal par le jeune deceu,
Hors de sa change se verra disarmé,
Arles ne monstres double soit aperceu,
Et Liqueduct et le prince embausmé.

VIII:68

The old Cardinal by a youth deceived
  Then change will find him disarmed
Arles, do not show the double is noticed
  And the aqueduct and the prince embalmed.

Shortly before his death Cardinal Richelieu was displaced by a court favourite, Cinq Mars. The prelate uncovered a plot made at Arles by Mars and the King's brother, the Duke of Orléans, with the Spanish king to depose the French king. The cardinal took the proof to the King, who had Mars executed. Richelieu died on a canal barge, hence 'Liqueduct' meaning 'led by water'. Richelieu's death was followed six months later by that of the King. Both their bodies were embalmed, as the last line states.

While France is in mourning, Philip IV of Spain attacks.

Au temps du dueil que le felin monarque,
Guerroiera le jeune Aemathien,
Gaule bansler perecliter la barque
Tenter Phossens au Ponant entretien.

X:58

At the time of mourning, the feline monarch
shall war against the young Aemathien,
France will quake, the ship in danger
Marseilles tried, a talk in the west.

When Louis XIII died (the mourning) and before the boy-king Louis XIV (Nostradamus called him 'Aemathien', the child of the dawn) could be crowned, the Spanish king, Philip IV, seized the opportunity to attack France. The attempt failed, but not before Marseilles almost fell into his hands. The 'talk in the west' would be the peace negotiations.

The new king, Louis XIV, was only five when he came to the throne and he reigned for 70 years, the most glorious epoch in all French history. He early realised that war was a fact of life, so he tried to ensure that wars were fought on someone else's territory, not his. To that end he kept his famous military engineer, Vauban, busy rebuilding the cities along his frontiers into impregnable fortresses. He then conquered further territories that strengthened those borders. He had canals dug; all the arts were encouraged so that they flourished. The living conditions of his people were raised so that truly he earned the right to be called the 'Sun King'. Unfortunately his last years ended in disaster, due to the exhaustion of the kingdom's continuous fighting.

Louis XIV strengthens the fortresses of his kingdom.

Les enemis du fort bien esloignez,
  Par chariots conduict le bastion,
Par sur murs de Bourges esgronnez,
  Quand Hercules battra l'Haemathien.

IX:93

The enemies of the fort will be kept distant,
  By wagons will be bought the bastions.
Of their height the walls of Bourges will crumble.
  When Hercules battles the bloody one.

In this quatrain is the prediction that Louis XIV would have the
wagons bring masonry to walls which would be reduced in height
now that artillery was becoming more efficient in smashing down
city walls. 'Hercules' here represents France, the bloody one her enemy.

Under Louis XIV, France enjoyed prestige and prosperity.

De brique en marbre seront les murs reduicts
  Sept et cinquante annees pacifiques,
Joye aux humains, renoué l'aqueduct,
  Santé, grands fruicts, joye et temps melifique.

X:89

From brick to marble will the walls be rebuilt
  Seven and fifty years of peace.
Joy to humans, the aqueduct renewed.
  Health, much fruit, joyful and mellifluous times.

A wonderful account of Louis XIV's reign. The aqueduct mentioned
was the Languedoc Canal, a herculean task. It took 15 years to build
at a cost of 34 million francs. The canal connects the Mediterranean
and the Atlantic Ocean. Whenever England imposed a blockade, it
was of inestimable value, transporting goods from the Mediterranean
to the Atlantic safe from enemy action.

20

Louis XIV prevents the relief of Rochelle.

L'entree de Blaye par Rochelle et Anglois
Passera outre le grand Aemathien
Non loing d'Agen attendra le Gaulois,
Secours Narbonne deceu par entretien.
IX:38

The entry of Blaye by Rochelle and the English
Shall pass beyond the great Aemathien.
Not far from Agen, will wait the French
Help from Narbonne, deceived by talk.

An incident early in Louis's reign when the English under Lord
Buckingham failed to relieve the Huguenots in Rochelle, then under
siege by the French forces.

The century from 1580 saw many changes in Europe.

En l'an cinqcens octante, plus et moins
On attendre le siecle bien estrange,
En l'an sept cens et trois (cieus tesmoins)
Que plusieurs regnes un a cinq feront change.
VI:2

In the year five hundred and eighty, more or less,
One shall await a strange century,
In the year seven hundred and three (skies as witness)
Many realms, one to five shall change.

Eight years after 1580, England defeated the Spanish Armada. Then
in 1603 the crowns of England and Scotland were united, allowing
Great Britain to become a world power. In 1703, Philip V, the
grandson of Louis XIV became king of Spain with its rich colonies.
This powerful combination threatened the rest of Europe, hence the
wars of the Spanish Succession.

Louis XIV revokes the Edict of Nantes. Europe ready for struggle.

Croix, paix, soubs un accompli divin verbe
L'Espaigne et Gaule seront unis ensemble
Grand clade proche et combat tresacerbe,
Coeur si hardi ne sera qui ne tremble.

IV:5

Cross, peace, made under the accomplished divine word
   Spain and France united together,
A great disaster nears, and combat furious,
   No heart so hardy that will not tremble.

The first line refers to the revocation of the Edict of Nantes so curtailing religious freedom in France. With Louis and his grandson Philip V on the thrones of France and Spain, the rest of Europe prepared for a desperate struggle.

War in Europe because Spanish princesses migrated to France.

Par mort la France prendra voyage à faire
Classe par mer, marcher monts Pyrenees.
Espaigne en trouble, marcher gen militaire,
Des plus grand dames en France emmenees.

IV:2

Because of a death France will make a voyage,
   The fleet by sea; marches over the Pyrenees
Spain in trouble, marches by military folk.
   Because the royal ladies were led away to France.

Philip V, grandson of Louis XIV, inherited the Spanish throne in 1700. Austria, England, Holland, Prussia and Savoy objected and united to support the Archduke Charles. The war in Spain lasted 12 years, during which the French fleet put to sea and French troops crossed the Pyrenees, all because Louis XII and Louis XIV married Spanish princesses.

22

Louis XIV lived a life of debauchery and carelessness.

> *Ce grand monarque qu'au mort succedera,*
> *Donnera vie illicite et lubrique;*
> *Par nonchalance à tous concedera,*
> *Qu'à la parfin faudra la loi Salique.*
>
> V:38

> The great monarch, successor by death
> Shall lead an illicit and debauched life.
> By nonchalance he will concede to all
> So that in the end the Salic law will fail.

Louis XV was five when he came to the throne, so Philip, the Duke of Orléans, became Prince Regent. He was a man of little ability. Continuous wars almost bankrupted the country. The king's indulging of his many mistresses did not help. Their interference in politics is the meaning in the last line, 'the Salic law will fail', i.e. rule by women.

Under the misrule of the Prince Regent, France shall change.

> *Coeur, riguer, gloire, le regne changera,*
> *De tous points contre ayant son adversaire,*
> *Lors France enfance par mort subjugera,*
> *Un grand Regent sera lors plus contraire.*
>
> III:15

> In heart, vigour and glory the realm will change,
> In all points contrary with his adversary,
> Then through death a child shall rule over France;
> The Great Regent, then will be very contrary.

The first line is contrasting the two previous reigns. The third line may allude to the suspicion that the boy-king's father, the Duke of Brittany, and grandfather, the Duke of Burgundy, had both been poisoned so that the Regent could exercise authority.

Louis XVI will have only nine peaceful years.

Neuf ans le regne le maigre en paix tiendra,
  Puis il cherra en soif si sanguinaire,
Pour lui grand peuple sans foy et loy mourra,
  Tué par un Beaucoup plus debonnaire.

II:9

Nine years shall the lean one keep the realm at peace,
  Then he shall fall into such a bloody thirst
That a great people without faith and law shall die
  Killed by one better than himself.

Now we come to the most tragic figure in modern history, the life and death of Louis XVI. He was a well-meaning, tolerant man always desirous of the best for his subjects. Unfortunately he did not have the ability to make decisions. Also, he suffered for the sins of his predecessors. A handsome man, he was faithful to his wife and thought the same of her. Louis could not decide policy; in 18 years he had 67 ministers and he could not anticipate events, surrendering only at the last instant. Democracy was working in Great Britain and the USA. Why not in France? But with every concession he made, the radicals wanted more, until eventually they took his life. He was a pacifist who was prepared to give his own life rather than others should shed their blood on his behalf – a sacrifice he was to make in vain.

Louis XVI put to death for his benevolence.

Le trop temps trop de bonté royale
  Fais et deffaicts prompt subit negligence,
Legier croira faux d'espouse loyalle.
  Lui mis à mort sa benevolence.

X:43

Too much of good times, too much royal bounty
  Feat and defeats, prompt sudden negligence

He will lightly believe his false wife loyal.
He will be put to death for his benevolence.

I have already explained this quatrain in describing Louis XVI.

Under Louis XVI high inflation lowers value of money.

D'escrit de Roy mumismes descriees,
  Et seront peuples esmuez contre leur roi
Paix, faict nouveau, sainctes loix empirees,
  Rapis onc fut en si dur arroi.
                                    VI:23

Despite the King, money will be devalued
  And the people will rise against their king,
A new peace will be made, holy laws made worse
  Paris was never in such disarray.

French people in the 1770s speculated in a Louisiana land scheme
which collapsed and caused the franc to be devalued. The rise against
the King was the French Revolution, when the Church was abolished
and a new constitution was adopted. Note: 'Rapis' here is an
anagram for Paris.

Nothing is changed, the public rule instead of the king.

Souz ombre saincte d'oster de servitude,
  Peuple et cité l'usurpera luy mesmes,
Pire fera par faux de jeune pute,
  Libre au champ lisant le faux proesme.
                                    V:5

Under the holy shadow of removing servitude,
  People and cities will themselves usurp power,
Worse will be done by the tricks of a young whore
  In a book in the fields reading a false promise.

This a description of the Revolution, which displaced royal power with one just as autocratic. After storming the Bastille the rabble took over governing Paris. The 'young whore' was the queen, Marie-Antoinette, who was not trusted after the affair of the diamond necklace. 'The false promise' was that given by the king when he promised not to escape from St Cloud, where the royal family were placed to be safe from harm.

The royal couple escape. Caught at Varennes and sent to Paris for trial.

De nuict viendra par le forest de Reines,
  Deux pars vaultort, Herne la pierre blanche,
Le moine noir en gris dedans Varennes,
  Esleu cap. cause tempeste, feu, sang tranche.

IX:20

By night, shall come through the forest of Reines
  Two partners, by a detour, Herne, the white stone,
The monk-king in grey in Varennes,
  The elected Cap. causing fire, blood slicing.

A very famous quatrain. The royal couple began to fear for their lives, particularly as the neighbouring sovereigns, concerned about their own thrones and lives, declared war on France. So disguised as predicted, the royal couple fled by coach eastwards towards Germany. At Varennes (a small village of only 700 today), the inn and storekeeper detained them pending advice from Paris. 'Herne' is an anagram for Queen; 'noir' is another for 'roi', king. 'Cap' is for 'Capet', the royal family name insultingly used by the revolutionaries for the king.

Louis XVI tried before a tribunal of 500, headed by the Comte de Narbonne.

Le parti solus mari sera mitré,
  Retour conflict passera sur le Tuille,
Par cinq cens un trahir sera tiltré,
  Narbon et Saulse par couteaux avons d'huille.

IX:34

The husband alone will be mitred,
  Return, a conflict, he shall pass over the Tuileries,
By five hundred, one traitor will be titled.
  Narbon and Saulse will have oil for knives.

A continuation of the last quatrain. Saulse was the mayor and inn-keeper of Varennes, who had detained the king. 'Narbon' was the titled Comte, who had been Louis's Minister for War, and now was the president of the 500 from Marseilles who attacked the Tuileries, putting the king under arrest. The 'mitre' was the headgear worn by all revolutionaries. The site of the Tuileries had been a quarry in Nostradamus's time.

The two lowest estates will be raised above the nobility.

Second et tiers qui font prime musique,
  Sera par roi en honneur sublimee,
Par grasse et maigre presque demi eticque,
  Rapport de Venus faulx rendra deprimee.

X:28

Second and third making the best music,
  Shall by the King be raised to top honours,
By the fat and thin ones and the half starved one,
  A false rumour about Venus shall pull her down.

Here we have a detailed prophecy of events and people involved in the French Revolution. Because of the hostility displayed by the nobility and clergy, two of the most powerful groups in France, towards the third estate, it constituted itself as a National Assembly and took one of the most active parts in the fomenting of the

27

Revolution. The King (Louis XVI) during this time was retained as 'ruler' of the country. Perhaps the most remarkable part of this prophecy is the clarity of the description of Mirabeau (the fat one), Danton (the lean one) and Marat (emaciated one), the three leading figures in the Revolution. 'Venus' would be Queen Marie Antoinette.

The Council of Three Hundred decide that the king shall die.

Trois cens seront d'un vouloir et accord,
  Qui pour venir par bout de leur attainte
Vingt mois apres tous et records,
  Leur Roy trahit simulant haine fainte.
V:37

The three hundred will be of one mind and accord,
  To come to bring about their ends,
Twenty months later by all records
  Their king, they shall betray by a false hatred.

The Council of Three Hundred, or the Legislative Assembly, after a period of deliberation ordered Louis XVI to stand trial for treason, trumping up a false charge.

The conspiracy to rob the king of his crown and life will be carried out.

Mort conspiree viendra en plein effect,
  Charge donnee et voyage de mort,
Esleu, crée, receu par siens deffaict,
  Sang d'innocence devant par remort.
VIII:87

The conspired death shall come to full effect,
  Charge given and a journey to death.
Elected, created, received by his own defeat,
  Blood of innocence, ahead of him in remorse.

The conspiracy to rob Louis XVI of his crown and life will be successfully carried out. The change to the position of the constitutional king and his flight to Varennes (journey to death) will be the cause of his death. He will be defeated by his own nation who earlier elected him. His innocent blood will later be a source of remorse to the French.

Louis XVI, Marie Antoinette and Madame Du Barry all beheaded.

Le regne prins, le Roy conjuera
La dame prinse à mort, jurez à sort,
La vie à Roine fils on desniera,
Et la pellix au sort de la consort.

IX:77

The Kingdom taken, the King will plot
The Lady taken to death, sworn by lot,
The life of the Queen's son is denied,
And the mistress shares the fate of the consort.

A most remarkable quatrain. Here Louis XVI, his queen, his son and his father's concubine are all sentenced to death, all of which we know occurred. The Queen being tried by jury is very interesting as there was no such thing in France previously. 'Pellix' in Latin means a mistress or concubine; Mme. du Barry was the mistress of Louis XV.

The execution of Louis XVI.

Par grand discord la trombe tremblera,
Accord rompu; dressant la teste au ciel;
Bouche sanglante dans le sang nagera,
Au sol la face ointe de laict et miel.

I:57

The trumpet shall tremble with a great discord,
An accord broken, raising the head to heaven

29

The bloody mouth shall stream blood,
   To the sun, the face that was anointed with milk and honey.

Prince de beauté tant venuste,
   Au chef menee, le second faict trahi:
La cité au glaive de poudre face aduste,
   Par le trop grand meutre le chef du Roi hai.
                                                VI:92

Prince of very comely beauty,
   Master of intrigue; to second place betrayed
The city of the knife shall burn the face with powder
   For so great a murder the king's head will be hated.

Both these quatrains describe the last moments of Louis XVI.
'Anointed with milk and honey' refers to that part of the coronation
ceremony before a king is crowned. 'The city of the knife' was
Paris, where the guillotine stood. 'The powder' was the quicklime
used to hasten the body's decay. When they realised what they
had done, the French hated themselves, the meaning of the last
line.

The fate of the Dauphin (Louis XVII) is uncertain.

La main escharpe et la jambe bandee,
   Louis puisne de palais partira,
Au mot du guet la mort sera tardee,
   Puis dans le temple à Pasques saignera.
                                                VIII:45

The hand in a sling and the leg bandaged
   The younger Louis will depart the Palace,
At the watchword, the death will be delayed,
   Then later at Easter in the Temple he will bleed.

Enfant sans mains, jamais veu si grand foudre,
   L'enfant royal au feu d'oesteuf blessé,

Au pui brises fulgures allant moudre,
Trois sous les chaines par le milieu troussés.

I:65

Infant without hands, never was lightning seen so great,
   The royal infant hurt playing tennis in the temple at
   Easter.
Bruised at the well, lightning strikes,
   Three trussed up in the middle under oaks.

The last two quatrains are assumed to be about the fate of Louis XVII or the Dauphin, Louis XVI's son. His fate is uncertain. He is said to have been placed under the care of a cobbler named Simon with indefinite orders as to the boy's treatment. Witnesses who saw the boy state that 'he had two tumours on his arms and swellings on both legs and at the back of the neck'. Officially, he died on 8 June 1795. In later years there were over 30 contenders to the throne, each claiming to be the unfortunate Dauphin. The last line in the second verse refers to the 'three' as the King, his queen and the Dauphin.

The French Assembly decide the Dauphin's fate.

Avant venu de ruine Celtique,
   Dans le temple deux parlementeront
Poingnard coeur, d'un monté au coursier et pique,
   Sans faire bruit le grand enterreront.

V:1

Before the coming ruin of France,
   Within the Temple, the Parliamentarians will decide the
   second.
Sword in the heart by one with a lance, mounted on a charger,
   Without making noise, the great one interred.

This is another version of the death of the Dauphin.

Robespierre, the silent one, elected to become a tyrant.

> *Esleu sera Renard ne sonnant mot,*
> *Faisant le saint public vivant pain d'orge,*
> *Tyranniser apres tant à un cop*
> *Mettant à pied des plus grands sur la gorge.*
>
> VIII:41

A Fox shall be elected who couldn't sing a note.
Made a public saint, living on barley bread,
Shall tyrannise over all, suddenly,
Putting his foot upon the throat of the greatest.

The French Revolution far exceeded the Russian one in savagery. Bitterly as a Frenchman, Nostradamus saw it all. This and the following quatrains paint these harrowing times, beginning with the most bloodthirsty monster of all, Maximilien Robespierre. The above verse needs no explanation, which came to pass just as our seer saw it.

Amid a bloodbath, Robespierre is guillotined, arms and legs broken.

> *Coq, chiens, et chats de sang seront repeus,*
> *Et de la playe du tyran trouvé mort.*
> *Au lict d'un autre jambes et bras rompus,*
> *Qui n'avait peur de mourir de cruelle mort.*
>
> II:42

Cock, dogs and cats will be filled with blood,
And with the wounds of the tyrant found dead
In the bed of another, with legs and arms broken.
He who was not afraid to die, dies a cruel death.

In this text the 'cock' means France and the 'dogs and cats' the rabble of the Parisian mob that tired of the bloodbath. In 16 days, 1;285 victims were guillotined. In a tussle with his enemies Robespierre was wounded and, for safety, he spent his last night in the Hôtel de Ville.

The tyrant, Robespierre, thought executing his victims a ritual.

Celui de sang reperse le visage,
  De la victime proche sacrifiee
Venant en Leo augure par presage,
  Mis estra à mort pour lors la fiancee.
                                              II:98

He that shall have his face sprinkled with blood,
  Of the victim close to be sacrificed
The Sun in Leo will be an augury by presage.
Then he shall be put to death for his promise.

The guillotining of his victims Robespierre considered a religious ritual and it was only a sudden revolt that brought about his own death, the meaning of the last line.

Nantes taken by revolutionaries, citizens put to the sword.

Des principaux de cité rebellee,
  Qui tiendront fort pour liberté ravoir,
Detrencher masles, infelice meslee,
  Cris hurlemens à Nantes; piteux voir.
                                              V:33

The principal men of the city shall rebel,
  Who will fight hard to recover their liberty;
These men cut up, unhappy disorder,
  Cries, howling in Nantes, piteous sight.

Nantes became the focus of Vendean resistance against the Republic. After being at first successful, the issue developed into a deadly conflict with no quarter given. When the Republicans put down the

33

revolt, everyone, including 'priests, women, old men and girls' died. A thousand men were guillotined while others were tied, face to face, naked, placed in boats then rowed to the middle of the Loire and scuttled. The dead bodies formed a barrier at the river's mouth.

The soldiers of the 'Bocage' rebel against the republic.

> *Du mont Aymar sera noble obscurcie,*
> *Le mal viendra au joinct de Saone et Rosne.*
> *Dans bois caichez soldats jour de Lucie,*
> *Qui ne fut onc un si horrible throsne.*
>
> IX:68

From Mount Aymar the noble obscured,
    The evil will come at the junction of the Saone and Rhone,
In the woods soldiers hidden on St Lucy's Day,
    When there was never so horrible a throne.

The City of Lyons lies at the junction of the rivers Saone and Rhone. St Lucy's day is 13 December. In 1793, the Vendean peasants rebelled against the Republic, and became known as the 'soldiers of the Bocage', or woodland fighters. 'Aymar' was known as 'la Montagne' (the Mountain) from his position as one of those Reds who occupied the upper seats in the Assembly. As a regicide he helped to obscure the greatest noble of all, the king.

Hot-air balloon invented and used in warfare for the first time.

> *Istra du Mont Gaulfier et Aventin,*
> *Qui par trou avertira l'armée:*
> *Entre deux rocs sera prins le butin,*
> *De sext mansol faillir le renommee.*
>
> V:57

Out from Mont Gaulfier and Aventine,
    Who, by the hole, will warn the army.

Between two rocks shall the booty be taken,
Of Sextus the celibate, his renown shall fail.

The hot-air balloon was invented by the Montgolfier (Mont Gaulfier) brothers and first used at the Battle of Fleurus in 1794, to observe the enemy's movements. The last two lines refer to Pope Pius VI (Sextus). When many of the Papal lands were taken by Napoleon on behalf of the French republic, he lost all credence.

Everything old will have new names: white will be black, old will be new.

Faux exposer viendra topographie
  Seront les cruches des monuments ouvertes
Pulluler secte, saincte philosophie
  Pour blanches, noirs, et pour antiques verts.
                                                    VII:14

Topography will come to be exposed as false,
  They will open the urns of the monuments,
Sects, holy philosophy will swarm,
  Whites be blacks and ancients be unripe.

In 1789 the old regional districts became known as departments. The urns and tombs of royalty (and Nostradamus's) were opened and the ashes scattered. Anti-Christian sects were encouraged and people were told to forget old ideas and to accept new ones as being the truth.

Holders of old ideas will be martyrs: clergy will be abolished.

En bref seront de retour sacrifices,
  Contrevenans seront unis à martyre,
Plus ne seront moines, abbes ne novices,
  Le miel sera beaucoup cher que cire.
                                                    I:44

Soon, the sacrifices will return
　Contraveners will be one with martyrs
There will be no more monks, abbots or novices.
　The honey shall be dearer than wax.

This quatrain refers to the abolition of Christianity. With no more burning of incense, 'honey shall be dearer than wax'. The constitution of 1790 declared the abolition of the clergy and of all ecclesiastical orders.

Pope Pius VI warned not to go to a city between two rivers.

Romain Pontife garde de t'approcher
　De la cité que deux fleuves arrouse,
Ton sang viendras aupres de là cracher,
　Toi et les tiens quand fleurira la rose.
　　　　　　　　　II:97

Roman Pontiff be careful of approaching
　The city watered by two rivers
You will spit your blood there
　You and yours when blooms the rose.

A warning to Pope Pius VI, who was taken prisoner by the French and kept at Valence at the junction of the Saone and Rhone rivers. He died as predicted, vomiting blood on 29 August 1799 in Spring 'when the roses bloom'.

When cloaks were worn to protect oneself, and anarchy prevailed.

Quand la lictiere du tourbillion versee,
　Et seront faces de leurs manteaux convers,
La Republique par gens nouveaux vexee,
　Lors blancs et rouges jugeront à l'envers.
　　　　　　　　　I:3

36

When the litters by the whirlwind are overturned,
And faces shall be covered with cloaks;
The Republic shall be vexed by the new people
Then Whites and Reds shall judge each other wrongly.

During the French revolution, when people met each other on the
streets, it was hard to tell friend from foe, so everyone wore a cloak to
hide their identity. Only the nobility were carried about in 'litters' so
they soon fell into disuse. The final two lines describe the confused
thinking of the times.

Napoleon gives his famous oration before taking Milan.

Avant l'assaut l'oraison prononcee,
  Milan prins d'Aigle par embusches, deceus,
Muraille antique par cannons enfoncee
  Par feu et sang, à mercy peu receus.

III:37

Before the assault, an oration shall be proclaimed;
  Milan, deceived, is taken in an ambush by the Eagle.
The ancient walls will be breached by cannon;
  By fire and blood, few will receive mercy.

Napoleon was famous for haranguing his troops before battle.
Here, he is termed 'the Eagle' and here is predicted the famous
oration he gave before taking Milan in his first Italian campaign
on 15 May 1796.

Napoleon invades the Po Valley and leads an Egyptian
expedition.

Grand Pau, grand mal pour Gaulois recevra
  Vaine terreur du maritin Lyon:

Peuple infini par le mer passera,
Sans eschapper un quart d'un million.

II:94

The great Po will receive great harm from the French.
Vain terror to the maritime Lion.
An infinite people will cross the sea
Without escape for a quarter million.

Naufrage à classe pres d'onde Adriatique,
La terre tremble esmeile sur l'air en terre mis,
Egypte tremble, augment Mahometique.
L'Herault soi rendre à crier est commis.

II:86

A fleet will be wrecked near the Adriatic shore
The earth trembles, rises into the air, then falls to earth,
Egypt trembles, Mahometism increases.
The herald is sent out to parley surrender.

Read together, these two quatrains predicted 245 years beforehand that most audacious exploit of Napoleon – the conquest of Egypt in his attempt to conquer the world. He had arrived back in Paris after his first two-year very successful campaign in Italy and conceived, in secret, his scheme. The five-man Directorate, to rid themselves of a dangerous, ambitious man, agreed. In four months he had his forces ready, with embarkation ports at Toulon, Genoa, Ajaccio and Civita Vecchia. England was the 'Maritime Lion' and Napoleon's brilliant victories outnumbered against the well-trained Austrian armies, gave England, the 'Lion', every cause to be alarmed.

When Nostradamus wrote of 'infinite people' he meant that the army would include scientific men of all kinds, such as architects and archaeologists. Remember it was these experts who found and realised the value of the Rosetta Stone. There is mention of a quarter-million men being marooned in Egypt because of the loss of the French navy, but Nostradamus might have included allies Napoleon had acquired. In stating that the Battle of the Nile took place in the Adriatic Sea, our prophet is in error. The Adriatic is, of course, an arm of the Mediterranean Sea. However, he was correct in writing that the battle occurred in shallow water when he used the word 'd'onde' (wave or surf). His terse description of the blowing-up of the French Admiral Bruey's flagship *L'Orient* was masterly. The mighty 120-gun ship caught fire, and when the flames reached the ship's powder magazine with its hundreds of barrels of gun-powder, the ship was blown to smithereens: 'into the air, then falls to earth.'

If Napoleon had been able to take the vital fortress of Acre, defended by British officers and Turkish troops, he would have gained great numbers of allies from Druse and Christian tribes, anxious to overthrow their Turkish masters. But his small army was short of food and racked with plague. As a last resort he sent a 'herald' to the British commander, Sir Sydney Smith, in an endeavour to bluff him into surrendering. But Sir Sydney was too shrewd, and Napoleon had no option but to return to Egypt.

The Directorate of three takes over ruling France.

Barbare empire par le tiers usurpé,
  Le plus grand part de son sang mettra à mort,
Par mort senile par lui le quart frappé,
  Pour peur que le sang par le sang ne soit mort.
                                                III:59

The Barbaric Empire will be usurped by the three.
  Its very best part will be put to death,
By death of old age he will stricken a quarter,
  For fear that blood by his blood, shall not die.

When Napoleon returned secretly by ship from Egypt to France, he found chaos reigning. His recent conquests in Italy had been lost and the French economy was in ruins. By a coup, he had the Directorate replaced by a consulate of three, with himself as first consul. The second line refers to the number of men who were to die in his future wars. The last line alludes to the fact that Napoleon was always afraid that he would not be able to found a dynasty and that his blood line would die out with himself.

39

The coup d'etat of the eighteenth Brumaire.

Lou grand eyssame se levera d'abelhos,
  Que non sauran don te siegen, venguddos;
De nuech l'embousque, lou gach dessous las treilhos
  Cuitad trahido per cinq lengos non nudos.

IV:26

The great swarm of bees shall arise,
  It shall not be known whence they come,
The ambush by night, the sentinel under the vine,
  The city handed over by five tongues not naked.

'The swarm of bees' was Napoleon's emblem. The five men the 'talkers' were bribed ('non nudos') to hand over Paris and some were members of the Directory. The coup was planned the night before it took place.

Napoleon's famous crossing of the Alps in his enemy's rear.

Gaulois par saults, monts viendra penetrer,
  Occupera le grand lieu l'Insubre,
Au plus profond son ost fera entrer,
  Gennes, Monech pouseront classe rubre.

IV:37

The French by leaps shall penetrate the Alps,
  To occupy the great plain of Lombardy,
And very deep he shall make his army go,
  Genoa, Monaco will repulse the Red Fleet.

In the year 1800 the dominant power in Europe was the Austrian Empire which, allied with England, was trying to force the Republic of France to restore the Bourbon dynasty. The fighting was on two fronts: in the Rhine valley, where the French General Moreau was later to win the Battle of Hohenlinden; and in the south, where

General Massena was hard pressed defending Monaco and Genoa. Napoleon decided to create a new army of 40,000 men from raw recruits.

With this new army he achieved the miraculous feat of crossing the Alps via the Great St Bernard Pass and falling on the Austrian rear. Meanwhile the British fleet was blockading Monaco and Genoa. Our seer called it the 'Red Fleet' because of the 'red' cross of St George on the British battle ensign.

When Napoleon assumes the crown, the Vatican will lose territory.

> *Par Mars contraire sera la monarchie,*
> *Du grand Pecheur en trouble ruineux,*
> *Jeune noir rouge prendra la Hierarchie,*
> *Les proditeurs iront jour bruineux.*
>
> VI:25

> With Mars contrary, the monarchy
> Of the great Fisherman will be in ruinous trouble
> The young red king will take the Hierarchy,
> The traitors will act on the day of Brumaire.

As Mars is the god of war, the first line means 'the fortunes of war are not favourable to'. 'The monarchy of the great Fisherman' is the Vatican. 'Noir' is an anagram for 'roi', or king. So the line means Napoleon, who incorporated the Papal states into the Cisalpine Republic. In the last line we have one of the newly created months, 'Brumaire'. On 18 Brumaire (9 November 1799) on his return from Egypt, the Directorate was dismissed and Napoleon was installed as first consul.

Napoleon will be more fire than blood. He will vex the Vatican.

> *Pau, nay, loron plus feu qu'à sang sera,*
> *Laude nager, fuir grand aux surrez,*

41

Les agassas entree refusera,
Pampon, Durance les tiendra enferrez.

VIII:1

Pau, nay, loron shall be more blood than fire,
 To swim in praise, great ones will shun surveys,
He will refuse the magpies entry.
 Pampon, Durance he will hold imprisoned.

The first three names are towns in France, but as an anagram they make up 'Napaulon Roy' (Napoleon Rex) which at one time was an acceptable title. In Provençal 'agassa' means a magpie, so here it stands for a harping priest. The last line stands for the two popes, Pius VI and Pius VII, both of whom were at times held prisoner.

Nostradamus wrote eight quatrains about Napoleon, more than anybody else and each verse has different aspects of his character.

Napoleon will rise from a common soldier to be an emperor.

De soldat simple parviendra en Empire,
De robe courte parviendra à la longue
Vaillant aux armes en eglise ou plus pire,
Vexer les prestres comme l'eau fait esponge

VIII:57

From a plain soldier he will come to an Empire
From a short robe he will come to the long,
Valiant in arms, to the Church much worse,
 He will vex the priests as water does a sponge.

From being a lowly lieutenant, Napoleon became an Emperor. As a consul he wore a short tunic then as an Emperor he wore a long gown. Brave in battle, from the outset he was the Church's deadly enemy, confiscating all the Church's estates except only the Vatican itself in Rome and some country residences.

42

All Europe will fear Napoleon. He will prefer foreign women.

Du nom qui onques ne fut au Roy Gaulois,
  Jamais ne fut un foudre si craintif,
Tremblant l'Italie, l'Espaigne et les Anglois,
  De femme estrangers grandement attentif.

IV:54

Of a name never held by a French king,
  There never was a thunderbolt so feared,
Be afeared, the Italians, the Spanish and the English,
  To strange women, he will be very attentive.

A self-explanatory description of Napoleon's character, including his love affairs. Josephine Beauharnais, Marie Walewska and Empress Maria Louisa were all foreign women.

With his barbaric name, Napoleon will become mankind's scourge.

D'un nom farouche tel profere sera,
  Que les trois soeurs auront fato le nom;
Puis grand peuple par langue et faict dira
  Plus que nul autre bruit et renom.

I:76

By a ferocious name he will be called
  So the three sisters will get it from fate.
Later to a great people, of words and deeds he will speak,
  More than any other, he will have fame and renown.

The ancient Greeks believed that before our birth, the three sisters of fate decide our future life, its tasks and destiny. The name 'Napoleon' in Greek is Neopolluon, which means the destroyer or exterminator. He was famous for his harangues to his troops before battle. He was also a man of great learning and could speak well on all subjects.

More of a butcher than a prince, Napoleon will cost his nation dear.

> *Un Empereur naistra pres d'Italie,*
> *Qui à l'Empire sera vendu bien cher;*
> *Diront avec quels gens il se ralie*
> *Qu'on trouvera moins prince que boucher.*
>
> I:60

An Emperor will be born near Italy,
  Who will cost the Empire dearly,
They shall say when his friends are seen
  He shall be found, less a prince than a butcher.

Ajaccio in Corsica can be said to be near Italy. Our seer had few good words to say for Napoleon.

Italy suffers devastation in the wars between France and England.

> *Milan, Ferrare, Turin, et Aquillee,*
> *Capue, Brundis vexés per gent Celtique:*
> *Par le Lion et phalange aquilee,*
> *Quant Rome aura le chef vieux Britannique.*
>
> V:99

Milan, Ferrara, Turin, and Aquilla,
  Capua, Brindisi shall be vexed by the French people
By the Lion and the eagle's phalange,
  When Rome shall have the old British chief.

The sense of this quatrain is that the cities named will suffer privations in the to-and-fro war between France and England (Lion) in the struggle for domination. The 'old British chief' was the Cardinal Duke of York, Bonnie Prince Charlie's brother, the last of his line, who died in Rome in 1807.

Napoleon, near Boulogne, plans the invasion of England, then turns to invade Austria.

Dedans Bologne voudra laver ses fautes,
  Il ne pourra au temple du soleil,
Il volera faisant choses si haultes,
  En hierarchie n'en fut oncq un pareil.

VIII:53

Within Boulogne he will want to wash sway his faults
  In the temple of the Sun, but he will be unable;
He will fly away to do very great things
  In the hierarchy he never had a parallel.

In his effort to cross the English Channel, Napoleon had his army rigorously equipped and trained on the beach sands at Boulogne until he had the finest troops in the world. Westminster Abbey, where British kings are crowned, is the traditional site where a Temple of Apollo once stood. If he had conquered England this is where, to become crowned king of England, he would have confessed his sins before God. But the destruction of the French fleet at Trafalgar had ruined those plans, so he set off to defeat Austria (to do great things) by a series of forced marches into the heart of Europe.

Two bad events simultaneously: sultans slain and Napoleon plagues the Vatican.

Les deux malins de Scorpion conjoinct,
  Le grand seigneur meutri dedans sa salle;
Peste à l'Eglise par le nouveau roy joinct,
  L'Europe basse et septentrionale.

I:52

The two evils of Scorpio together,
  The grand Seignior murdered in his room,
Plague to the Church by the new king
  Of lower and northern Europe.

Then two evil planets of Scorpio are Mars and Saturn, which were in conjunction in 1807. The grand Seignior, Sultan Selim III of Turkey, was murdered the following year. Napoleon had now been made Emperor and had defeated Austria and Prussia (lower Europe) and Russia (Septentrionale). He had restored Catholic faith in France at the time of his coronation and now had the new Pope Pius VII imprisoned.

Troops bivouac around besieged Rome and Vatican looted of treasures and territory.

> *Tout à l'entour de la cité,*
>   *Seront soldats loges champs et villes;*
> *Donner assaut Paris, Rome incité,*
>   *Sur le pont lors sera faicte grande pille.*
>   V:30

All around the great city,
   Will be soldiers lodged in fields and villages
Then will Paris assault, Rome aroused.
   On the Pope will be made great pillage.

'Paris' here stands for France. This verse foretells either of the two French sackings of Rome in 1797 and 1808, when much treasure and territory were taken from the Vatican.

Wellington with a new army drives the French from Spain.

> *Bien contigue des grans monts Pyrenees,*
>   *Un contre l'aigle grand copie addresser*
> *Ouvertes veines, forces exterminees,*
>   *Comme jusque à Pau le chef viendra chasser.*
>   IV:70

Very near the great Pyrenees mountains
   One against the Eagle will raise a great army,

Veins will be opened, forces exterminated,
As far as Pau the chief will chase them.

Wellington, then Sir Arthur Wellesley, was the British general throughout most of the Peninsular War. It ranged back and forth for some five years, sapping many much-needed men and materials from the Russian campaign then being fought by the French. Pau here is not the River Po but the town in southern France.

Joachim Murat failed his brother-in-law Napoleon, who never forgot.

Gaulois qu'empire par guerre occupera,
 Par son beau frere-mineur sera
  trahi.
Par cheval rude voltigiant trainera
 Du fait le frere long temps sera hai.

X:34

A Frenchman who shall occupy an Empire by war,
 By his brother-in-law shall be betrayed,
He will be dragged by an untrained horse,
 For the fact the brother will long be hated.

Created King of Naples by the Emperor Napoleon, Joachim Murat proved himself an energetic capable administrator. He married Napoleon's youngest sister, Caroline Marie-Annoncide. Six feet tall, he was a dashing cavalry man. Fearless, like Napoleon, he bore a charmed life in battle. From beginning to end he fought in nearly all Napoleon's great battles. Napoleon was jealous he made Murat a king; and Murat was jealous he made Napoleon an Emperor. Murat was not really a traitor. As King of Naples, Murat had declared that only native Neapolitans could enjoy civil or military stipends. This annoyed Napoleon until the breach was healed by Caroline. Murat went with the Grand Army to Moscow. When that retreating army reached the banks of the River Niemen, Napoleon hastened on to Paris, leaving Murat in charge. But

when his charge had reached secure quarters he resigned his post
to tend to his own kingdom. Napoleon objected, and made it
known publicly.

Eugène de Beauharnais served his country and stepfather well.

L'enfant du grand n'estant à sa naissance,
  Subjugera les hauts monts Apennins,
Fera trembler tous ceux de la balance,
  Et de monts feux jusques à mont Senis.
                                    V:61

The infant of the great one who was not at his birth
  Shall subdue the high Alpine mounts,
He will make all those under Libra tremble,
  And mount fire as far as mount Cenis.

Eugène de Beauharnais was Josephine's son and Napoleon's stepson,
and a soldier of no mean ability. But his administrative talents were
more valuable. So he was made Viceroy of the Kingdom of Italy. He
fought several battles in the Swiss Alps.

The Grand Army advances on Russia. Moscow taken and burnt.

Amas s'approche venant d'Esclavonie,
  L'Olestant vieux cité ruinera,
Fort desolee verra sa Romanie,
  Puis la grand flamme estaindre ne scaura.
                                    IV:82

A mass will approach near Slavonia,
  The Destroyer will ruin the old city,
Very desolate will be his Romania,
  Then the great flame will be unextinguishable.

As Napoleon's Grand Army was composed of various units from all parts of Europe so it could be said to be 'a mass'. 'Olestant' and 'Napoleon' both mean 'Destroyer'. The scorched earth policy adopted by the Russians would be the cause of 'very desolate' scenery. Moscow's defenders torched their city and there were no means of putting the flames out.

The plundered Vatican pleased at the French misfortunes in Russia.

Terroir Romain qu'interpretoit augure,
Par gent Gauloise par trop sera vexée;
Mais nation Celtique craindra l'heure,
Boreas classe trop loing l'avoir poussée.

II:99

The Roman land in which the augur did interpret
For the French people shall be very vexed.
But the French nation shall fear the hour
The North wind has driven the fleet too far.

There were many Italian soldiers in the Grand Army so many of its principalities would be annoyed at the French reverses in Russia because no plunder would fall to them. The last line means the North Wind (Boreas) has driven the French fleet (army) too far.

Napoleon fights the Battle of Waterloo 100 days after his return from Elba.

Au mois troisiesme se levant le soleil,
Sanglier, Liepard au champ Mars pour combattre,
Liepard laissé, au ciel extend son oeil.
Un aigle autour du Soleil voit s'esbattre.

I:23

In the third month, at sunrise,
The Boar and the Leopard on the field of Mars will fight,

The Leopard wearily to heaven lifts his eye,
    Sees an Eagle playing around the Sun.

Here is the prediction that three months after his return from Elba Napoleon would fight the Battle of Waterloo. The 'Boar' is the Prussians, the 'Leopard' is the British and the 'Eagle' is Napoleon, or the French. The British on the northern part of the battlefield had to look into the sun, the meaning of the last two lines.

Waterloo was a matter of life or death to the French.

Le sol et l'aigle an victeur paroistront,
    Response vaine au vaincu l'on asseure;
Par cor ne cris harnois n'arresteront,
    Vindicte paix par mors si acheve à l'heure.

I:38

The Sun and the Eagle will seem victorious
    A vain response will be made to the vanquished,
Neither bugle nor cries will stop the soldiers
    Revenge, or peace by death if made in the hour.

In the course of battle, Napoleon (eagle) on the offensive appeared to be winning, but with the arrival of Marshal Blucher and his army instead of Marshal Grouchy, the day was lost. The last line describes Napoleon's Imperial Guard, who were thrown in as a final attempt for victory and who fought to the last man.

Wellington wins at Waterloo. Imperial Guard fights to the end.

Prest à combatre fera defection,
    Chef adversaire obtiendra la victoire,
L'arriere garde fera defension,
    Les deffaillans mort au blanc territoire.

IV:75

The ready to fight will desert,
  The chief adversary will obtain the victory,
The rear guard will make a defence
  The failures dead in a white country.

Marshall Grouchy was the deserter in the first line. He failed to proceed to the battlefield at the sound of gunfire. However, Napoleon himself fled the field when the battle was lost. Wellington was the 'chief adversary'. The Imperial Guard is implied in the third line, for they fought to the last man to allow Napoleon to escape. Those that flee when a battle is lost will find the rear filled with white flags of surrender.

The French people are loyal to Napoleon but Paris demands his resignation.

Un dubieux ne viendra loing du regne,
  La plus grand part le voudra soustenir,
Un Capitole ne voudra point qu'il regne
  Sa grande charge ne pourra maintenir.
                                    VI:13

A dubious one will not go far from the realm,
  The greater part will wish to uphold him,
The Capital will not want him to reign
  His great seat he will not be able to keep.

After Napoleon's downfall he still had the support of the French people, but Paris, under pressure from the victorious allies, demanded he resign, which he did in favour of his infant son.

As the defeated French army leaves Paris, the allies enter with fixed bayonets.

Les longs cheveux de Gaule Celtique,
  Accompagnez d'estranges nations

Mettront captif la gent Aquitanique,
  Pour succomber a leur intentions.

III:83

The long hairs of Celtic France
  Accompanied by foreign nations
Will take captive the Aquitainic people
  To force them to yield to their intentions.

After Napoleon's defeat the 'long hairs', the old aristocracy, and the Allies, 'the foreign people', compelled the French; 'the Aquitainic People', to accept the Bourbon kings again.

The happy, easy-going, Louis XVIII, King of France, died loving good food.

Heureux au regne de France, heureux de vie
  Ignorant sang, mort, fureur et rapine
Par non flateurs seras mis en envie,
  Roi desrobé, trop de foi en cuisine.

X:16

Happy in the realm of France, happy in life
  Ignorant of blood, death, anger and rape,
By no flatterers shall be envied
  King robbed, too much faith in the kitchen.

The antithesis to the previous monarch, Louis XVIII was a renowned gourmet. His flattering name was 'Louis le Desire'.

An inhuman tyrant is succeeded by a kindly savant in Louis XVIII.

Cent fois mourra le tyran inhumain;
  Mis à son lieu, scavant et debonnaire,
Tout le Senat sera dessoubz sa main,
  Faché sera par malin themeraire.

X:90

A hundred times the inhuman tyrant shall die,
   In his place, a savant and kindly man,
All the Senate will be in his hand,
   He shall be vexed by a malicious scoundrel.

The first line predicts the thoughts Napoleon might have had at St Helena. Louis XVIII was no warrior, but rather a scholar who revelled in his library and the arts. And as he left the running of the country to the Senate he was popular with them. The 'scoundrel' was Louvel, who assassinated the heir presumptive to the throne, the Duke de Berry. Of Louvel we will learn more later.

The lame diplomat, Talleyrand, could arrange anything against his sovereign.

   Celui qu'en Sparte claude ne veut regner,
   Il fera tant par voie seductive;
   Que du court, long, le fera araigner,
   Que contre Roi sera sa perspective.
                                        VI:84

   The lame man who could not rule in Sparta
      Shall do much in a way seductive,
   By hook or by crook he shall arrange
      That which is against his king and his prospects.

Charles Maurice Talleyrand-Perigord (1754–1838) was lame. 'Claude' means lame. In ancient Sparta, deformed children were put to death at birth. In 1807 he was Napoleon's Great Chamberlain but he resigned and thereafter plotted against his former master. Against the wishes of the French people, he advised the Allies to recall the Bourbons in 1814 when Napoleon resigned in favour of his infant son, Napoleon II, then the King of Rome and later the Duke of Reichstadt.

Did Napoleon's son and heir, Napoleon II, die of leprosy?

Le mineur fils du grand et hay prince,
 De lepre aura à vingt ans grande tache,
De deuil sa mere mourra bien triste et mince,
 Et il mourra là où tombe cher lache.

IV:7

The minor son of the great and hated prince
 Will be very marked by leprosy before he is twenty,
His mother will die of grief, very sad and thin,
 And he will die when his skin falls from his bones.

Napoleon had adopted Josephine's son, Eugène, before his own son, Napoleon II, was born, so the first line could be in order. At his birth, Napoleon created him King of Rome, but upon Napoleon's downfall this title was abolished, so his grandfather, the Emperor of Austria, made him the Duke of Reichstadt. He was a serious, studious boy with a taste for a military life. His biographers wrote that he developed consumption, now known as tuberculosis. In this highly infectious disease, in which the blood vessels of the lungs are infected, the victim bleeds to death, not as in leprosy where the flesh is destroyed. Napoleon Francis Joseph Bonaparte died in Vienna in 1831, in his twenty-first year.

The Duke of Berry assassinated by Louvel, on 13 February.

Chef de Fosan aura gorge coupee,
 Par le ducteur du limier et laurier;
La faict patre par ceux de mont Tarpee,
 Saturn in Leo, 13 de Fevrier.

III:96

The chief of Fossano will have his throat cut
 By the keeper of the bloodhounds and greyhounds,
The deed will be committed by those of the Tarpean Rock,
 Saturn in Leo, 13th February.

The Duke of Berry was Louis XVIII's nephew and, after his brother Charles, heir to the throne. As he assisted his wife into a coach after attending a performance at the Paris Opera House, the Duke was stabbed by a Republican sympathiser named Louvel, an employee in the Royal Stables. This is a remarkable prediction, for the deed occurred on 13 February 1820 just as foreseen by Nostradamus.

The gift from heaven, the birth of the Comte de Chambord.

> *Un serpent veu proche du lict royal*
> *Sera par dame nuict chiens n'abayeront;*
> *Lors naistre en France un Prince tant royal,*
> *Du ciel venu tous les Princes verront.*
> IV:93

A serpent will be seen near a royal bed
  By a lady at night, the watchdogs will not bark,
Then there will be born a Prince so royal
  That all the princes will see him as a gift from Heaven.

The Duchess of Berry gave birth to a son seven months after her husband's death. Its legitimacy was challenged by the Duke of Orleans (the serpent) who had the right of room entry. The birth of a grandson to King Charles X was a cause of much rejoicing, so the child was called 'a gift from Heaven'.

The desired Comte de Chambord, always in exile fearing his enemies.

> *Le arbre qu'estoit par long temps mort seché*
> *Dans une nuict viendra à reverdir;*
> *Cron Roy malade, Prince pied estaché,*
> *Craint d'ennemis fera voiles bondir.*
> III:91

The tree that was a long time dead and withered
  In one night will be revived again
The old king unwell, the Prince with a club foot,
  Fear of their enemies will make them hoist sail.

The miraculous 'tree' was the House of Bourbon which, when the
Duchess of Berry gave birth to her posthumous son, was revived
overnight. The Prince's foot was deformed when he fell from a horse
at the age of four. He went with his grandfather into exile in 1830,
ever pursued by his enemies.

Louis-Phillippe will have seven peaceful years, then students will
end his reign.

> Sept ans sera Philip fortune prospere
>   Rabaissera des arabes l'effaict,
> Puis son midi perplex rebours affaire,
>   Jeune ogmion abismera son fort.
> IX:89

For seven years shall Philip's fortune prosper
  He shall humble the Arab's efforts
Then in middle age, complex reverse affairs
  Young Ogmion will pull down his strength.

As foretold, all went well with the king for seven years. He
completed the conquest of Algeria, thereby humbling 'the Arab's
efforts'. In the middle of his reign things went awry. Students in a
prestige school rioted and demanded a republic and in 1848
one came.

Louis-Phillippe will have no rest in his reign, but he will conquer in
Africa.

> Plus ne sera le grand en faux sommeil,
>   L'inquietude viendra prendre repoz;

56

Dresser phalange d'or, azur et vermeil,
Subjuger Affrique le ronger jusques oz.
                                    V:69

No more will the great one sleep falsely,
    Restlessness will overcome repose,
He will dress a phalange in gold, blue and vermilion.
    He will subdue Africa and gnaw it to the bone.

In his reign Louis had no rest and was always on the go. He fought a popular war in Algiers. He accepted the Revolutionary colours of red, white and blue. To make the army popular he took to dressing his soldiers in spectacular colours.

Greed and use of force was Louis-Phillippe's undoing.

Par avarice, par force et violence
    Viendra vexer les siens chef d'Orléans,
Pres Saint Memire assault et resistance.
    Mort dans sa tante diront qu'il dort léans.
                                    VIII:42

By avarice, by force and violence
    The chief of Orleans will come to vex his own;
Near St Memire, assault and resistance.
    Dead in his tent, they will say he sleeps there.

Louis-Phillippe had an excessive love of money, to the nation's disadvantage. The end of his rule came when a group of students revolted at St Meri's college (not Memire, but very close). After living in exile in England for 12 years, his servants one morning would not disturb him because they thought he was sleeping.

To bolster Louis-Phillipe's popularity, Napoleon's remains are returned to Paris.

> *Du Triumvir seront trouvé les os,*
> *Cherchant profond thresor aenigmatique,*
> *Ceux d'alentour ne seront en repos.*
> *Ce concaver marbre et plomb metallique.*
>
> V:7

Of the Triumvir will be found the bones,
  When seeking a profound and enigmatic treasure.
Those around will not be at rest.
  This recess of marble and metallic lead.

Louis-Phillippe, to revive his waning popularity sought and obtained Napoleon's remains from St Helena. 'The Triumvir' was Napoleon, as the first Consul when the Consulate ruled France.

Louis Bourbon Condé, the last of his line, was found strangled in 1830.

> *De nuict dans lict le suspresme estranglé,*
> *Par trop avoir sejourné, blond esleu;*
> *Par trois l'empire subrogé exanché,*
> *A mort mettra carte, et pacquet ne leu.*
>
> I:39

By night in bed, the last great one strangled,
  For being too involved with the fair elect,
By the three, the Empire enslaved and replaced,
  Put to death, neither paper nor packet read.

In 1830, the last of the Condés, Louis Bourbon Condé, was found strangled in his bed for the support he was giving to the Comte de Chambord, heir to the throne. 'The three' were the regimes that followed: Louis-Phillippe, the Republic and Napoleon III. Condé is said to have made a will in the Comte's favour, the meaning of the last line, which was not acted upon.

The Comte de Chambord's marriage to the Duke of Tuscany's daughter.

Du vray rameau des fleurs de lys issu,
Mis et logé heretier de Hetrurie;
Son sang antique de long main tissu
Fera Florence florir en l'armoire
V:39

Issued from the true branch of the Fleur de Lys,
Placed and lodged as the Etruria
His ancient line woven by many hands
Will make the armorial bearings of Florence flower.

The Comte de Chambord's legitimacy was challenged at his birth by
the Duke of Orleans. 'Etruria' stands for Tuscany, where he married
the Grand Duke's daughter, with whom he lived in exile.

The Comte de Chambord's death ended a possible civil war in France.

Long temps au ciel sera veu gris oyseau,
Aupres de Dole et de Touscane terre;
Tenant au bec un verdoyant rameau,
Mourra tost grand et finera la guerre.
I:100

A long time in the sky shall be seen a grey bird
Near Dole and the land of Tuscany
Holding in his beak a green branch.
Dying too soon, he will finish the war.

In exile the Comte de Chambord lived at Dole near Venice and
finally at Modena in Tuscany. Before he could have children, he died,
thus avoiding a future war for the French throne.

The Comte de Chambord, the true contender, is challenged by the Comte de Paris.

> *Quand dans le regne parviendra le boiteux*
> *Competiteur aura proche bastard;*
> *Lui et le regne viendront si fort roigneux,*
> *Qu'ains qu'il guerisse son faict sera bien son tard.*

III:73

When into the realm comes the lame one
   The competitor will be a close bastard;
He and the realm will be so strongly trimmed
   So that before it is cured, it will be too late.

The Comte de Chambord, the true contender, was challenged by the Comte de Paris (the competitor). Chambord came to an agreement with the French people but the intervention of the Franco-Prussian War meant the agreement lapsed, the meaning of the last line (also of the last line of quatrain I:100).

Napoleon III's son was christened by the Pope at birth.

> *Au Roy l'augur sur le chef la main mettre,*
> *Viendra prier pour la paix Italique;*
> *A la main gauche viendra changer la sceptre,*
> *De Roy viendra Empereur pacifique.*

V:6

On the King's head the augur will place his hand
   To pray that peace will come to Italy;
To the left hand he will change the sceptre,
   From a king, he will become an Emperor of peace.

The Prince Imperial was a godson of the Pope, who christened him in December 1858. As his own father had been Louis, King of Holland, the change that was to take place was from King to Emperor.

Napoleon III escapes death when a bomb damages the Paris Opera House.

Jusques du fonds la grand arq demolue,
Par chef captif l'ami anticipe;
Naitre de dame front face chevelue,
Lors par astuce Duc à mort attrappé.
V:9

At the base of the demolished arch
The chief captured, the friend will anticipate,
Born of a lady with face and forehead covered with hair,
Then by astuteness the Duke will escape death.

When he was a young man, Napoleon was an Italian Nationalist sympathiser, but on becoming an Emperor his former comrades felt betrayed. So four of them attempted to assassinate him as he left the Opera House by blowing it up. Orsini, the leader, was arrested. 'The friend' Pieri was also arrested. As these two were captured before the explosion, Napoleon (or 'the Duke') must have saved his life by being cautious.

Emperor's life saved by four unknown bystanders.

Un chef Celtique dans le conflict blessé,
Aupres le cave voyant siens mort abbatre,
De sang et playes et ennemis pressé,
Et secours par incogneus de quatre.
V:10

A French chief wounded in a conflict
Near a show cellar, sees his own struck dead
The blood and wounds and enemies pressing
And he will be saved by four unknowns.

A continuation of the previous quatrain. Four bystanders saved the life of the Emperor, who was wounded, by shielding him with their

61

bodies. The second line means the Emperor saw his subjects struck dead.

Napoleon III will proclaim peace everywhere, yet his wars will cost one third of a million casualties.

> *Sous un la paix par tout sera clamee,*
> *Mais non long temps, pillé et rebellion,*
> *Par refus ville, terre et mer entamee,*
> *Morts et captifs le tiers d'un million.*
>
> I:92

> Under the One, peace for all will be proclaimed,
> But not for long, then pillage and rebellion.
> For refusal, villages, by land and sea will be assaulted.
> Dead and captured, a third of a million.

Napoleon's reign began peacefully, but at the end there were wars. The 'refusal' in the third line was the demand he made on the Germans, that led to the disastrous Franco-Prussian War of 1870. The *Encyclopaedia Britannica* quotes the same figure of casualties as Nostradamus predicted.

When Dame Fortune smiled, Napoleon III smiled: when she frowned, disaster struck.

> *Où tout bon est, tout bien Soleil et Lune,*
> *Est abondant, sa ruine s'approche,*
> *Du ciel s'advance vaner ta fortune,*
> *En mesme estat la septiesme roche.*
>
> V:32

> When all is well, 'tis good, Sunshine and Moonshine
> Is abundant, your ruin is approaching,
> The heavens are advancing to change fortune
> Into the same state as the seventh rock.

This quatrain describes Napoleon III as he was at the height of his good fortune in 1867, the year of the Exposition Universelle. Three years later, the Franco-Prussian War brought disaster. The 'Seventh Rock' is mentioned in St John's Revelation.

The Grand Duke of Tuscany loses his throne when France invades northern Italy.

Dela les Alpes grande armée passera,
  Un peu devant naistra monstre vapin,
Prodigieux et subit tournera,
  Le grand Tosquan à son lieu plus propin.
                                        V:20

A great army will pass over the Alps,
  A little while before a wretched monster is born,
Prodigious and sudden he shall return
  The grand Tuscan to his own native land.

In 1859 Napoleon III crossed the Alps with a great army. The 'vapid monster' was the rise of Italian Nationalism, which was to eventually turn all the petty states into modern Italy. The Grand Duke of Tuscany was Austrian born and as a result of the war he lost his throne, so had to return to his 'native land'.

The People of Tuscany will weep as their Duke departs his realm.

Pleure Milan, pleure Luques, Florence,
  Que ton grand Duc sur le char montera,
Changer le siege pres de Venise s'advance,
  Lors que Colonne à Rome changera.
                                        X:64

Weep Milan! Weep Lucca! and Florence
  When your Grand Duke mounts upon his chariot

To change his seat as it advances near Venice.
When at Rome the Colonnas will change.

When the Grand Duke left Tuscany to Napoleon III, he in turn gave it to his ally Victor Emmanuel, who made Florence his temporary capital until he acquired possession of Rome. When he did so, the influence of the Colonna family was broken, the meaning of the last line.

Napoleon III, having beaten two regimes for his throne, furls his colours at Sedan.

Par le decide de deux choses bastars
Nepveu du sang occupera le regne,
Dedans Lectoure seront les coups de dars,
Nepveu par peur plaire l'enseigne.

VIII:43

By the fall of the two bastard things
The Nephew of the blood shall occupy the realm;
Within Lectoure shall be blows by darts
The Nephew through fear shall fold up his colours.

'The two bastard things' were the Orleans monarchy and the Second Republic. 'Lectoure' is an anagram for Le Torcey, a suburb of Sedan, where Napoleon ordered a flag of truce to be hung on its Cathedral, then later, the citadel. He surrendered at Douchery, some two miles away from Le Torcey.

After the bloody war the royal palace burns. Minor cities are loyal to their Emperor.

De feu celeste au royal edifice
Quand la lumiere du Mars deffaillira;
Sept mois grand guerre, mort gent de malefice.
Rouen, Eureux au Roy ne faillira.

IV:100

Celestial fire from the Royal Palace
    When the light of Mars is a failure,
Seven months will the war last, dead the malific people.
    Rouen, Evreux, will not fail their king.

At the end of the 'seven month' war the Commune of Paris rebelled and set fire to the Royal Palace, the Tuileries. The two cities named refused to admit defeat by denying billets to the German soldiers.

By surrendering, Napoleon III will lose his empire.

Au deserteur de la grand forteresse,
    Apres qu'aura son lieu abandonné;
Son adversaire fera si grand prouesse
    L'Empereur tost mort sera condamné.
                                        IV:65

To the Deserter of the great fortress
    After he has abandoned his place
His adversary will display great prowess.
    The Emperor will be condemned to death.

For surrendering, the Commune of Paris condemned Napoleon to death. 'His adversary', of course, was the Germans who certainly did show 'great prowess'.

Lorraine and Alsace were ceded to Germany, Normandy and Picardy occupied.

Des lieux plus bas du pays de Lorraine,
    Seront des basses Allemagnes unis,
Par ceux du siege Picards, Normans du Maisne,
    Et aux cantons ce seront reunis.
                                        X:51

The lowest places of the country of Lorraine
    Will be united with lower Germany,
For those, the seats of the Picards, Normans of Maine
    And the cantons will be re-united.

Lorraine and Alsace were ceded to the newly created Germany while the other areas mentioned were under German occupation pending settlement of peace terms.

As a result of war, the Rhine is no longer a French river.

Le Celtique fleuve changera de rivage
    Plus ne tiendra la cité d'Agripine,
Tout trasmue ormis le vieil langaige,
    Saturne, Leo, Mars, Cancer en rapine.
VI:4

The French river will change its banks,
    And no more come to the City of Cologne;
All will be changed except the old language.
    Saturn, Leo, Mars, Cancer in rapine.

With the surrender of Alsace-Lorraine, the Rhine no longer flowed through French territory. There was now only a land frontier with Germany. However, the people still spoke the same languages.

The Empress Eugenie rose from poverty to rule with a vile temper.

De terre faible et pauvre parentele,
    Par bout et paix parviendra dans l'Empire;
Long temps regner une jeune femelle,
    Qu'oncques en regne n'en survint un pire.
III:28

Of poor land and poor family
    By effort and peace she shall attain to the Empire,
A long time a young female shall rule,
    Such a one ruling was never worse.

In 1853, the Emperor Napoleon III married the young and beautiful Eugenie de Montijo, the daughter of an impoverished Spanish landholder. It was said of her that she began by being the futile woman and ended by being the fatal woman. She had the most vile temper that intimidated both the Emperor and the palace servants. She used her position to have her say on state policy.

The Prince Imperial christened by Pope Pius IX.

Index et poulse parfondra le front
    De Senegalia le comte à son filz propre;
Les Myrnarmee par pluieurs de prins front,
    Trois dans sept jours blesses morts.

                                        X:8

With index finger and thumb will the forehead be wet
    By the Comte de Senegalia's proper son;
The Venus with many by the prince's brow.
    Three in seven days wounded to death.

Napoleon's son, the Prince Imperial, was born on 15 June 1856. His godfather was Pope Pius IX, the son of Count Mastoi Ferretti of Senegalia. 'La Myrnarmee', or Venus, was the Empress Eugenie. The last line was some contemporary event not recorded.

The Prince Imperial has a miraculous escape from death.

Feu, couleur d'or de ciel en terre veu,
    Frappé du haut nay, faict merveilleux;
Grand meutre humain; prince du grand nepveu.
    Morte d'expectacles eschappe l'orgueilleux.

                                        II:92

Fire, the colour of gold from heaven to earth will be seen
  The high-born struck, a marvellous event.
Great human slaughter, prince of the great nephew.
  A spectacle of death; the proud one escapes.

This verge describes a narrow escape from death, during the Franco-Prussian War, when a shell struck the ground near the Prince Imperial and exploded. The last two lines describe the battle scene. The prince was later killed in South Africa while serving with the British Forces when his unit was overwhelmed by Zulus.

Crown Prince Ferdinand dies a horrible death when his horse bolts.

L'aisné royal sur coursier voltigeant,
  Picquer viendra si rudement courir,
Gueulle, lipee, pied dans l'estrain pliegnant,
  Trainé, tire, horriblement mourir.

VII:38

The eldest royal prancing on a steed
  Shall spur, and, running wildly shall bolt,
Open mouth, foot in stirrup, crying,
  Dragged, worn out, dying horribly.

Crown Prince Ferdinand, the heir of Louis-Phillippe, was thrown and dragged by his horse on 13 July 1842 and died a cruel death.

Captain Dreyfus wrongly accused and sent to Devil's Island.

Tard arrivé l'execution faicte,
  Le vent contraire lettres aux chemin prinses;
Les conjurez quatorze d'un secte;
  Par le Rousseau semez les entreprinses.

I:7

The arrival late, the execution a fact,
  The wind contrary, letters intercepted en route,
The fourteen conspirators of one kind,
  By Rousseau shall these enterprises be made.

Captain Alfred Dreyfus, a Jewish officer, was court-martialed and condemned to Devil's Island on the charge of having given the Germans military secrets in 1894. Five years later a retrial again found him guilty. A further inquiry was ordered. It found that the minister in charge of the trial, Waldeck-Rousseau, an anti-semite, had used false evidence. Note that Nostradamus predicted the true name of the minister.

The coming of the flaming comet, Pope Leo XIII, was predicted by two prophets.

Durant l'estoille chevelue apparente,
  Les trois grans princes seront faits enemis,
Frappés du ciel paix terre trembulente
  Pau, timbre undans serpens sur le bord mis.
                                        II:43

During the hairy star's appearance
  The three great princes will be enemies.
Struck from heaven will be the shaky peace on earth
  Pau, the winding Tiber, serpents cast upon the shore.

On his coat of arms Pope Leo XIII had a flaming comet, and it was during his reign that the Triple Alliance was formed in 1881 between Germany, Austria and Italy (three princes) against France. The fact that disturbed the peace was the formation of the opposition Triple Entente. This situation led to the 1914 Great World War. Besides Nostradamus, the Irish bishop St Malachy gave Leo XIII the motto 'the light in the sky'. His family crest was a comet of gold on an azure field.

General Charles de Gaulle will rule all other monarchs.

> *Hercules roi de Rome et d'Annemarc,*
> *De Gaule trois guion surnommé:*
> *Trembler l'Italie et l'un de Sainct Marc,*
> *Premier sur tous monarque renommé.*
>   IX:33

Hercules! king of Rome and Denmark,
   De Gaulle his surname, three times chief
Be afraid Italy and the one of St Mark
   First over all the renowned monarchs.

Nostradamus always used 'Hercules' as the patron saint or spirit of France. A most remarkable prophecy for our times. Under the Treaty of Rome, its signatories surrendered many of their sovereign powers to the Community. The French president, Charles de Gaulle took the dominant role for five years until he resigned as president in 1969. As Italy had been a republic since 1944 there was no king in Italy. Denmark was also kingless from 1964, although Nostradamus has pre-dated its accession, which did not occur until 1973. So for five years he was 'king' over Italy and Denmark. 'The one of St Mark' was Pope John XXIII, who was the Cardinal of Venice before becoming pope, St Mark of Venice being his principal cathedral.

Charles de Gaulle was 'three times leader'. *1:* He led the French resistance forces against the Germans. *2:* He reformed the Republic and became its president. *3:* He became the leader of the European Economic Community.

There are further quatrains dealing with General de Gaulle and Marshal Pétain, but I will deal with them under the heading of World Wars One and Two, and future events.

2

BRITISH HISTORY

Being near neighbours has caused the fates of both Great Britain and France to be closely interwoven, usually in the roles of rivals or enemies, particularly since the times of Nostradamus. The Island fortress united early and since 1603 has shown a united front to Europe and the World, and so has been more fortunate than France, which was divided into petty principalities, each a possible pretender for the throne. It took the reigns of the kings Henry II to Louis XIV, or a period of over 150 years, to consolidate the monarchy and to be able to compete on somewhat equal terms with Great Britain, only to start from scratch again after the French Revolution. So in the scramble for overseas colonies, Great Britain has had the advantage, and it was only with the advent of Louis XIV that France was able to enter the race by sending out explorers, missionaries and settlers to colonise, when the race was almost over. However, the following quatrains prove how much Nostradamus was aware of the events that were to come in Great Britain.

England will become a mighty empire, moving big armies by land and sea.

Le grand empire sera par Angleterre,
  Pempotam des ans plus de trois cens

Grandes copies passer par mer et terre;
Les Lusitains n'en seront contens.

X:100

England will become a great Empire.
'All powerful' for more than three hundred years
Great armies shall pass by land and sea.
The Portugese will not be pleased.

This could not be a truer prophecy for England and the British
Empire. I believe the 300 years started from when Portugal presented
the Indian city of Madras as a dowry to Charles II in 1662. Then in
1947 Great Britain granted India and Pakistan their independence,
thus spanning a period of 285 years. This figure also ties in with the
previous quatrain. The last line means that Portugal, although being
among the first to acquire colonies, was forced to be allied with
England to keep them. When Great Britain gave up her Empire,
Portugal was soon forced to follow suit. So England and Portugal
were allies by necessity.

**In 290 years Great Britain shall have seven forms of government,
not so France.**

Sept fois changer verez gent Britannique
Taints en sang en deux cents nonante an.
Franche non point par appuy Germanique.
Aries double son pole Bastarnien.

III:57

Seven times you will see the British people change
Tainted in blood in 290 years
France not so with German support.
Aries will double his Bastarnan pole.

Nostradamus did not name the starting date, so if we take the year
1603 we can get the following table.

72

1: *Elizabeth I of the House of Tudor*	*−1603*
2: *The House of Stuart; James I & Charles I*	*1603−1649*
3: *Oliver Cromwell; The Commonwealth*	*1649−1660*
4: *The Restoration; Charles II & James II*	*1660−1688*
5: *The Glorious Revolution; William and Mary,*	
Queen Anne	*1688−1714*
6: *The House of Hanover*	*1714−1901*
7: *The House of Saxe-Coburg-Gotha*	
(Windsor)	*1901−*

This list includes eight years too many, no serious error for our seer, so it appears that the present dynasty will be the last to rule Great Britain. Nostradamus was a keen supporter of royalty and that is the reason for the word 'tainted' in the second line, reminding us of the execution of Charles I.

There has been no satisfactory explanation for the meaning of the last line. The use of 'Aries' could mean its astrology reading. Others say the use of the word 'Pole' could be a reference to the fact that the last war started over the invasion of Poland by the Germans. The cost of surviving the two world wars started by Germany has been the British Empire's downfall.

The British Empire gave the world the 'Pax Britannica'.

> *Le regne humain d'Angleterre geniture,*
> *Fera son regne paix union tenir,*
> *Captive guerre demi de sa closture,*
> *Long temps la paix leur fera maintenir.*
>
> X:42

The humane reign of the English offspring
　　Will make their reign of peaceful union hold;
Captive will be war half in its prison,
　　A long time their peace will hold.

A predicted tribute to the 'Pax Britannica' and the civilising influence the British have had on the world. The second line refers to the fact that the English, Scots and Welsh have been able to maintain a peaceful union for so long.

Mary I loses Calais to France; the besieged behave barbarously.

> *Entrée profonde par la grand Roine faicte,*
> *Rendra le lieu puissant inaccessible;*
> *L'armee des trois lyons sera deffaicte,*
> *Faisant dedans cas hideux et terrible.*
>
> VII:16

The very deep entry made by the great Queen
  Will render the place powerful and inaccessible;
The army of the three lions will be defeated,
  Doing inside, hideous and horrible deeds.

This quatrain recalls the capture of Calais by the Duke of Guise in 1558, after being in English hands for 200 years. As England's gateway to Europe, it had been of the utmost importance to English commerce.

Humble as a princess, Elizabeth I as a queen will display great vanity.

> *Jour que sera par Roine saluee,*
> *Le jour apres le salut, la priere,*
> *Le compte fait raison et valuee,*
> *Par avant humbles oncques ne feut si fiere*
>
> X:19

The day that she shall be greeted as Queen
  The day after being saluted at evening prayers,
The account being settled and paid
  She that was humble before, now never so proud.

To many as a princess, Elizabeth I was low. Low became high.

Le naturelle à si hault, hault non bas,
Le tard retour fera marris contens,
Le recloing ne sera sans debats
En empliant et perdant tous son temps.

X:84

The illegitimate girl so high, not low
    The late return will make the grieved pleased
The reconciled shall not be without debate
    In employing and wasting her time.

Pope Paul IV had declared Princess Elizabeth illegitimate, thus unfit to reign. The English Catholics took the same line, hence the meaning of the last two lines. The second line refers to the Protestants persecuted under Mary I.

Phillip II of Spain woos Elizabeth I of England.

Apres le Roy du sud guerre parlant
L'Isle Harmotique le tiendra à mespris,
Quelques ans bons rongeant un et pillant,
Par tyrannie à l'Isle changeant pris.

X:36

After the king of the south has talked war
    The harmonious Isle will despise him,
Some good years gnawing and pillaging
    By tyranny on the Isle, its values will change.

The first two lines express Elizabeth's attitude when Phillip II expressed a wish to marry her, and the last two lines when her sailors were plundering Spanish ships and possessions in the New World.

The rejected Elizabeth I triumphed more as she grew older.

La dechassee au regne tournera,
Ses ennemis trouvés des conjurez
Plus que jamais son temps triomphera,
Trois et septante à mort asseures.

VI:74

The pursued will return to reign
Her enemies will be found to be conspirators:
Ever more her time will be triumphant,
Three and seventy, to death will be very sure.

When Henry VIII died, his two elder children reigned before Elizabeth. Before coming to the throne she was under constant guard; Admiral Seymour was beheaded for leading a plot to place her on the throne. Throughout her glorious reign of 45 years, conspirators were ever plotting. The last line predicts her death at 70 in 1603 (her 70 and the three).

Howard, Raleigh and Essex 'singe the King of Spain's beard'.

Devant le lac ou plus cher fut getté
De sept mois, et son host desconfit,
Seront Hispans par Albanois gastez
Par delai perte en donnat le conflict.

VIII:94

Before the lake where the great treasure was cast
Of seven months and its host discomfited
The Spanish by the Albions plundered
By delay in giving battle.

In the first line, the word 'cher', or dear, becomes treasure or valuables. 53 galleons and warships were in the port of Cadiz when the English seamen attacked in 1596. 'Cadiz' comes from an Arabic word meaning an enclosed space.

The great Spanish Armada ships tower over the small English ships.

Voille gallere voil de nef cachera,
  La grande classe viendra sortir la moindre
Dix naves proches le tourneront poulser,
  Grande vaincue unis à foi joindre.

X:2

The galley's sail shall hide the ships
  The Great Armada shall bring out the little ones,
Ten ships approach, turnabout repulsed,
  The great one vanquished, united to join in faith.

This is a prophecy of the defeat of the Spanish Armada in 1588, when the huge galleons towered over the English ships, and their arrival brought the English out of their channel ports.

The marriage of Francis II of France and Mary, Queen of Scots.

Premier fils, veufve, mal'heureux marriage
  Sans nul enfans, deux isles en discorde,
Avant dixhuict incompetant aage,
  De l'autre pres plus bas sera l'accord.

X:39

The first son, a widow, an unhappy marriage,
  Without children, two isles in discord.
Before eighteen, an immature age,
  Of the other, even less the accord.

In the chapter on French history I have used this quatrain before because it affects both France and Great Britain seriously. Mary, a cousin of Queen Elizabeth, married Francis II, who ruled France for only a few months, dying before he was 18 years of age. Mary had been brought up in the French court as a Roman Catholic. On her return to rule over Scotland, she was determined to force Protestant Scotland to change their religion to hers. As England under Elizabeth

77

was also Protestant, this caused the 'isles to be in discord'. The next French king, Francis's brother Charles IX, was only nine when he came to throne. He was betrothed at eleven to Elizabeth of Austria, hence the meaning of the last line. A most accurate prediction.

Mary, Queen of Scots and the mysterious 'casket letters'.

Lettres trouvees de la roine les coffres,
Point de subscit sans aucun nom d'autheur
Par la police seront caché les offres.
Qu'on ne scauru qui sera l'amateur.

VIII:23

Letters found in the queen's casket
No signature, no name of the author
By the police will be hidden the offers
So no one will know who the admirer was.

Some commentators refer this quatrain to Cardinal Rohan and Marie Antoinette, but the word 'police' places it in Britain, in what is known as the 'casket letters'. They were documents relating to the murder of Lord Darnley in 1567. They were produced before commissions in London and York and then they vanished.

In 1604, the crowns of England and Scotland were united to form Great Britain.

Le Grand Bretagne comprinse d'Angleterre,
Viendra par eaux si fort à inonder.
La ligue neufve d'Ausonne fera guerre,
Que contre eux ils se viendront bander.

III:70

Great Britain will comprise England,
Will be by water a great inundation,
The new league of Italy will make war,
So that they will band against them.

After Elizabeth I died, Mary Queen of Scots' son, James VI, king of Scotland, also became James I of England in 1603. The English, the Welsh and Scots all became united as Great Britain. In 1607, Somerset and Bristol experienced severe flooding. The previous year the Holy Alliance was formed. 'L'Ausonne' stands for Italy. His popular brother Arthur dying, the tragic Charles I came to the throne. A cultured man of expensive tastes, he believed in the 'divine right of kings' – that is, God ordained kings, so therefore they could do no wrong.

Charles I's troubles began on his wedding day.

> *Le divin mal surprendra le grand prince,*
> *Un peu devant aura femme espousee.*
> *Son appuy et credit à un coup viendra mince,*
> *Conseil mourra pour la teste rasee.*

I:88

Divine wrath shall overtake a great prince
A short time before he marries a woman,
His support and credit shall be reduced,
For counsel he shall die because of the shaven head.

On his wedding day, Charles I decreed that laws against the Catholics should cease. Parliament challenged this right, and his right to raise money for war. Oliver Cromwell was the 'shaven head'.

King Charles I driven away, Archbishop Laud burnt, but Charles accepted by the Scots.

> *Du regne Anglois l'indigne dechassé,*
> *Le conseiller par ire mis bas à feu,*
> *Ses adherans iront si bas trasser,*
> *Que le bastard sera demi receux.*

III:80 or III:82

The unworthy of the English realm shall be driven away,
    The counsellor through anger shall be burnt,
His adherents shall stoop so low
    That the bastard will almost be received.

So desperate had he become for money, Charles had allowed his 'counsellors' Lord Stafford to be beheaded and Archbishop Laud to be burnt. He himself was the 'unworthy'. 'His adherents' were the Scots, who sold him back to Parliament half-(demi)heartedly.

Oliver Cromwell will talk well and be elected commander of the army.

Le grand crier sans honte audacieux,
    Sera ecleu gouverneur de l'armee;
La hardiesse de son contentieux,
    Le pont rompu, cité de peur pasmee.
                    III:79 or III:81

The great prayer, shameless and audacious
    Shall be elected commander of the army;
The boldness of his disputed claims,
    The city of Pontefract shall faint from fear.

When Civil War broke out, the king, supported by the nobility, was initially successful. Oliver Cromwell quickly saw that if Parliament was to succeed it would need better trained and equipped troops. These he undertook to provide. Having done so, he now proceeded to lead them and, being a good tactician, he was soon the supreme commander. 'The Broken Bridge', or Pontefract, held out valiantly for the king before falling to the Parliamentary forces.

Of unknown origin, Oliver Cromwell will ruthlessly attain
power.

> *Plus macelin que roi en Angleterre,*
> *Lieu obscure nay par force aura l'empire;*
> *Lasche sans foi, sans loi seignera terre,*
> *Son temps approche si presque je soupire.*
> VIII:76

More a butcher than king in England,
  Born in an obscure place, by force he shall gain the
    Empire,
Lewd, no faith, no laws, the earth shall bleed;
  His time nears so close that I sigh.

After the king's demise, Cromwell, as Lord Protector, was king in all
but name. Nostradamus had no love for anyone who would kill his
anointed king. A puritan, Cromwell was an enemy of the seer's faith,
without his ideas of faith or laws.

Charles I shall die in his shirt in the Tower of London.

> *La forteresse aupres de la Tamise*
> *Cherra par lors le roi dedans serré,*
> *Aupres du pont sera veu en chemise*
> *Un devant mort, puis dans le fort barré.*
> VIII:37

The fortress near the Thames
  Shall fall; then the king who was kept within
Shall be seen near the bridge in his shirt
  Before death, then kept barred in the fort.

A most true, vivid, account of Charles's death borne out by a
contemporary woodcut of the event. The 'bridge' was the then
London Bridge. It will feature again when we discuss Winston
Churchill.

Parliament, financed by merchants, condemn Charles to death.

> *Gand et Bruxles marcheront contre Anvers;*
> *Senat de Londres mettront à mort leur Roi*
> *Le sel et vin lui seront a l'envers*
> *Pour eux avoir le regne en dessarroi.*
>
> IX:49

Ghent and Brussels shall march against Antwerp;
  The Senate of London shall put their king to death.
Salt and vine shall be against him
  By them the realm will be in disarray.

The first line tells of a contemporary European event. Parliament had formed itself into a court to try the king. 'Salt and wine' stands for the merchants, who paid most of the taxes and had most to gain by a Parliamentary victory. Nostradamus blamed them for the Civil War in the last line.

Cromwell will lose at Dunbar until the Scots leave the high ground.

> *La bande foible le terre occupera,*
> *Ceux du haut lieu feront horribles cris,*
> *Le gros troupeau d'estre coin troublera,*
> *Tombe pres D'nebro descouvert les escrits.*
>
> VIII:56

The weak band will occupy the land,
  Those above shall make horrible cries
The great flock in the outer corner in trouble,
  At the fall near Edinburgh the scripts will be found.

A forecast of the Battle of Dunbar, where the Scots held the high ground making 'horrible cries'. 'On the right corner', Cromwell was almost in a state of siege, with many sick and short, of supplies. Then sensing victory, the Scots attempted a charge downhill and

Cromwell's well disciplined force made short work of them. Dunbar is just a little east of 'D'nebro' (Edinburgh) where the 'escrits', the city archives, fell into Cromwell's hands.

At the Battle of Worcester, Charles II will vanish, then seven years later return, to no word of 'yes'.

Sur la minuict conducteur de l'armee
   Se sauvera subit esvanoui,
Sept ans apres la fame non blasmee.
   A son retour ne dira oncq oui.

X:4

At midnight the leader of the Army
   Shall save himself, vanishing suddenly;
Seven years later, his fame unblemished
   At his return, no word of 'Yes'.

In 1651, the future King Charles II, after the battle of Worcester, was forced to flee in disguise. Seven years later, after Cromwell's son's resignation, he was invited to take the throne. The former cries of 'yes' were forgotten.

The Great 1665 Plague of London.

Le grand peste de cité maritime,
   Ne cessera que mort ne soit vengée
Du juste sang par pris damné sans crime,
   De grand dame par feincte n'outragée.

II:53

The great plague of the maritime city
   Shall not cease until the death be avenged
Of the just blood, taken and damned without crime.
   The great dame outraged by pretence.

The sense of this quatrain is that the great plague was sent to the maritime city, London, as retribution for the execution of Charles I, who Nostradamus believed was unjustly executed.

The Great Fire of London in three times twenty and six.

Le sang du juste à Londres sera faute,
  Bruslés par foudres de vingt trois les six,
La Dame antique cherra de place haute
  De mesme secte plusieurs seront occis.

II:51

The blood of the just will be wronged
  Burnt by the fire of three time twenty and six.
The ancient Dame will fall from her high place,
  Of the same sect many will be killed.

The theme in both these two last verses is that London would suffer plague in 1665, then fire in 1666 for the death of Charles I. The 'antique Dame' was the statue of the Virgin Mary atop the spire of old St Paul's cathedral, which toppled into the flames of the wooden cathedral.

Judges and the well-to-do flee the plague in London.

Le juste à tort a mort l'on viendra mettre
  Publiquement en ce millieu estaint;
Si grande peste en ce lieu viendra naistre,
  Que les jugeans fouir seront constraint.

IX:11

The just will be wrongfully put to death
  Publicly taken out of the middle of society.
So great a plague will be born in that place
  That the judges will be forced to flee.

84

Here Nostradamus again says that the crime of regicide carries a penalty, so the Great Fire and plague were retributions sent by God. Here all the judges and civil dignitaries are forced to flee the flames.

The Scots defeated. Ten years' Commonwealth rule. The Stuarts restored.

De l'Aquilon les efforts seront grands,
    Sur l'ocean sera la porte ouverte
Le regne en l'isle reintegrande,
    Tremblera Londres par voille descouverte.

II:68

The Northerners will make great efforts
    On the ocean, the gate will be open.
The reign in the Isle will be restored
    London will be scared at the discovery of sail.

First we have the Scots' attempt to have the Stuarts restored when the British navy temporarily lost command of the sea, 'the ocean gates were open'. In the last two lines we have the restoration of the Stuarts in the person of Charles II, during whose reign the Dutch raided the Medway, not distant from London.

William III and James II duel for the British crown.

Le blond au nez forche viendra commettre
    Par le duel et chassera dehors;
Les exilez dedans fera remettre
    Aux lieux marins commettant les plus fors.

II:67

The Blond and the fork-nosed shall be committed
    To a duel and chase him off,
The exiles shall be restored
    Making the marine place much stronger.

Here 'the Blond', William III, is duelling the 'fork nosed', James II, for the throne. The British Protestant 'exiles' can now return home. The final line means that now that the two fleets of England and Holland are combined, the King has greater command of the sea than before.

Thirty Londoners conspire against James II and elect William of Orange.

Trente de Londres secret conjureront,
   Contre leur Roi sur le pont entreprinse,
Lui, satalites la mort degousteront
   Un Roi esleu blonde, natif de Frize.

IV:89

Thirty Londoners will secretly conspire
   Against their king; the enterprise being on the sea.
He and his satellites will dislike death.
   A king elected, native of Friesland.

William of Orange insisted that those who supported him should sign a paper. William sailed with a fleet (sea enterprise). The ones in the third line are James II and his adherents, who fled rather than fight. William III was blond and was born on Friesland, a Dutch island.

William and Mary II, by promising to uphold the Anglican church, win the crown from her brother.

La soeur aisnée de l'isle Britannique,
   Quinze ans devant le frere aura naissance;
Par son promis moyennant verrifique,
   Succedera au regne de balance.

IV:96

The elder sister of the British Isles
  Shall be fifteen, before her brother is born;
By her promise being verified
  She shall succeed to the realm of the Balance.

Mary II, co-sovereign with her husband William II, was born 22 years before her half-brother, but she was 15 when her father remarried the Catholic Anne of Modena, their child James being born six months after his father became king. Mary and William promised to uphold the Act of Supremacy establishing the Church of England as the state religion.

Louis XIV aids the Stuarts by landing troops in Ireland.

Le Roy Gaulois par la Celtique dextre,
  Voyant discorde de la grande Monarchie
Sur les trois pars fera florir son sceptre
  Contre la Cappe de la Grand Hierarchie.
                                                    II:69

The French king on the Celtic right
  Seeing the discord of the Great Monarchy
Of the three leopards will flourish his sceptre
  Against the head of the great Hierarchy.

Realizing his opportunity, Louis XIV gave support to his fellow Catholic king, James II, and gained temporary control of the sea and landed troops in Ireland. But William, by regaining mastery of the sea, was able to defeat them. Later Louis, when his grandson became king of Spain, together with him sought unsuccessfully to drive William III from his throne.

James and William contend for the British crown, but he who desires the Anglican title wins.

> *Regne en querelle aux freres divisé*
> *Prendre les armes et le nom Britannique*
> *Tiltre Anglican sera guard advisé*
> *Surprins de nuict, mener à l'air Gallique.*
> VIII:58

A kingdom divided between quarrelling brothers
  To take the arms and British name
The Anglican title will be advised to be on guard.
  Surprised at night, carried into French air.

James III, known in history as the Old Pretender, and William III were brothers-in-law; the one prepared to accept the 'Anglican Title' won the throne, the other was 'carried into French air'. This quatrain has been applied to Edward VIII and his abdication, but I am sure this is its correct place because of the 'Anglican Title'.

The first of the Hanoverian kings ascends the throne.

> *Apres viendra des extremes contrées*
> *Prince Germain, sur le throsne d'ore*
> *En servitude et par eaux recontrées*
> *La dame serve, son temps plus n'adore.*
> II:87

Later there shall come from a distant land
  A German Prince on a golden throne;
Slavery and the waters shall meet,
  The lady serving, her time not much adored.

George I was the German prince of the 'distant land', invited to sit on the 'golden throne' of Great Britain. The lady of the last line is Britannia, who ruled the waves, who was responsible for both slavery and its abolition. Britannia's ships transported most of the world's merchandise, but now always more and more of it goes by air, so now 'her time [is] not much adored'.

Bonnie Prince Charlie will cause the English alarm when he invades England.

Soubs le terroir du rond globe lunaire,
  Lors que sera dominateur Mercure;
L'isle d' Escosse fera un luminaire,
  Qui les Anglois mettra à deconfiture.
                                    V:93

Under the territory of the round lunar globe
  When there is domination by Mercury,
The Scotch isle will produce a leader
  Who will put the English into confusion.

Bonnie Prince Charlie was the nearest to fulfilling this role when, in 1745, he advanced south to Derby before retreating back into Scotland.

The dying Nelson wins the Battle of Trafalgar.

Entre deux mers dressera promontoire,
  Que plus mourra par le mords du cheval;
Le sien Neptune pliera voille noire,
  Par Calpre et classe aupres de Rocheval.
                                    I:77

Between two seas stands a promontory
  He will later die by a bite of a horse.
Proud Neptune will furl the black sail;
  The fleet near Gibraltar and Rochelle.

Trafalgar is a cape between two bays (seas). The French Admiral Villeneuve, after his return from being a prisoner of war, was murdered by a Mameluke servant with a horse-bridle. 'The black sail' was the British flag of mourning for Lord Nelson. 'Calpre' is the Straits of Gibraltar and 'Rocheval' is Gibraltar itself.

At Trafalgar the combined Franco-Spanish fleet split into three parts.

> *De mer copies en trois parts divisees,*
> *A la seconde les vivres failliront;*
> *Desesperez cherchant champs Helisees*
> *Premier en breche entrez victoire auront.*
>
> IX:97

> At sea, the fleet will divide into three parts
> The second will fail the living,
> Desperate they shall seek the Elysian Fields;
> The first in the breach shall obtain the victory.

The Franco-Spanish fleet formed into a long line which was split into three parts by Nelson advancing two lines of ships each one behind the other. The surviving British Admiral, Collingwood, was the first to 'breach' the enemy line, thus being the victor.

Wellington at Waterloo awaits evening or Blucher.

> *Au mois troisiesme se levant soleil*
> *Sanglier, Liepard au champ Mars pour combattre;*
> *Liepard laissé, au ciel extend son oeil,*
> *Un aigle autour du Soleil voit s'esbattre.*
>
> I:23

> n the third month at the rising of the sun
> The Boar and the Leopard in the field of Mars fight;
> The Leopard weary, lifts his eyes to heaven
> Sees an eagle around the sun.

I have used this quatrain before in French history; however, I am using it again to fill a gap. Here the 'Boar' is Blucher, the 'Leopard' is Wellington, while the 'Eagle' is Napoleon. 'The third month' is a reference to the 100 days since Napoleon's escape from Elba.

After Trafalgar and Waterloo, Great Britain will be at her peak of power.

> *Apres combat et bataille navale*
> *Le grand Neptune à son plus haut befroi;*
> *Rouge adversaire de peur deviendra pasle*
> *Mettant le grand ocean en effroi.*
>
> III:1

After the combat and naval battle
   The great Neptune will be in his highest steeple,
The red adversary will wax pale with fear
   Putting the ocean in fright.

After the land battle at Waterloo and the naval battle at Trafalgar, Great Britain was at the height of her power, or 'highest steeple'. 'The red adversary' was Revolutionary or Napoleonic France.

Victoria reigned for 64 glorious peaceful years, good times for her subjects.

> *De brique en marbre seront les murs reduicts*
> *Sept et cinquante annees pacifiques,*
> *Joye aux humains renoué l'aqueduct,*
> *Santé, grands fruicts joye et temps melifique.*
>
> X:89

From brick to marble will the walls be rebuilt,
   Seven and fifty peaceful years
Joy to mankind, the aqueduct renewed,
   Health, ample fruits, joyful and mellifluous times.

For the most part, Queen Victoria's reign was a time of great prosperity. The country changed for the better, with better health and education plus greater opportunities for her people. They travelled further, quicker, cheaper and in more comfort. 'The aqueduct renewed' would be the Suez Canal, which had existed in Pharaonic times, but only from the Nile to the Red Sea instead of, as now, from the Mediterranean to the Red.

This quatrain has been used before for Louis XIV. Both monarchs reigned more than the 57 years and conferred great prosperity on their peoples.

British and French Empires weakened by the USA's later entry into both wars.

> *Le grand Neptune du profond de la mer*
> *De gent Punique et sang Gaulois meslé*
> *Les Isles à sang pour le tardif ramer,*
> *Plus lui nuira que l'occult mal celé.*
>
> II:78

The Great Neptune of the depths of the sea
The people of mixed African and French blood,
The Isles bloody because of the tardy stayer
Will be harmed more than the hidden evil.

'Great Neptune' and 'the Isles' are Great Britain. The second line is the French Colonial empire. The 'tardy stayer' was the USA, whose late entry into both World wars weakened both powers, in manpower and economically, and, as the last line says, this 'hidden evil' was more harmful than Hitler's submarines or secret weapons.

After George V dies, London shall demand the throne from Edward VIII.

> *Le jeune nay au regne Britannique,*
> *Qu'aura le pere mourant recommandé*

92

Icelui mort Londres donra topique
  Et à son fils le regne demandé.
                          X:40

The young man born to the realm of Great Britain
  Whom his dying father has recommended
Once dead, London shall give a topic
  And to his son demand the throne.

Because of his wife's divorce, Edward VIII will lose the crown.

Pour ne vouloir consentir à divorce,
  Qui puis apres sera cogneu indigne,
Le Roi des Isles sera chassé par force
  Mis à son lieu que de roi n'aura signe.
                          X:22

For not wanting to consent to the divorce
  Which later will be deemed unworthy,
The king of the Isles will be chased away by force
  Put in his place, one who has no sign of a king.

This is another prophecy that Edward VIII would lose his throne on
account of Mrs Simpson being a divorcee.

The grand old Lion, Winston Churchill, will be by London
defeated, by fear re-elected.

Pres d'un grand pont de plaine spacieuse,
  Le grand lion par forces Cesarees
Fera abattre hors cité rigoureuse
  Par effray portes lui seront reserees.
                          I:33

Near a great bridge on a spacious plain
  The grand Lion by imperial forces

Will then be pulled down rigorously
For fear, the gates will be for him unlocked.

A wonderful prediction of the 'grand Lion' Winston Churchill. The 'great bridge' was the old London Bridge, which is surrounded by a 'spacious plain'. 'Pulled down' aptly describes his parliamentary defeat in 1945 and 'unlocked gates' his return to power the following election, 'for fear' when the Russians turned hostile, and put up the Berlin Wall, forcing the Allies to use an 'air lift' to supply their forces in Berlin.

Industrial troubles will cause Great Britain to join the Common Market.

Dedans les Isles si horrible tumulte,
  Bien on n'orra qu'une bellique brigue
Tant grand sera des predateurs l'insulte,
  Qu'on se viendra ranger à la grand ligue.
                                        II:100

Within the Isles there will be so great a tumult
  That nothing will be heard but the clashing of factions
Great will be the insults of the robbers
  That all will arrange to join the great league.

When World War Two was over, the demobilised troops were determined that no more would they live in pre-war poverty. They were going to have a world fit for heroes to live in, so they demanded the highest rates of pay, especially as work was plentiful. But inflation eroded their savings, so they began endless strikes. So bad did things become that the politicians joined the Common Market in the hope of improving their economy and thus reducing unemployment.

Great Britain, Denmark and Holland will waste money joining the Common Market.

> *Le second chef du regne d'Annemarc,*
> *Par ceux de Frise et l'Isle Britannique*
> *Fera despendre plus de cent mille marc*
> *Vain exploiter voyage en Italique.*
> VI:41

The second chief of the realm of Denmark
  With those of Frisia and the British Isles
Will spend more than 100,000,000 marks
  Vainly exploiting a way to Italy.

'The second head of Denmark' is its Prime Minister, or its Finance Minister. 'Frisia' stands for Holland, so with Great Britain, the three countries, in becoming members of the EEC will waste their money trying to trade with another member, Italy.

Of the descendants of convicts deported to Australia, a king will arise to make their laws.

> *Entre plusieurs aux isles deportés,*
> *L'un estre nay à deux dents en la gorge;*
> *Mourrant de faim les arbres esbroutés*
> *Pour eux neuf Roy, nouvel edict leur forge.*
> II:7

Among the many deported to the Isles
  One shall be born with two teeth in the mouth,
By those dying of hunger, the trees will be browsed
  For them, a new king making for them new edicts.

'The isles', Australia, Tasmania and Norfolk Island, were all first settled by convicts from Great Britain. In the semi-deserts of Australia many have died of starvation and the aborigines do eat leaves off trees. For many years now, the British sovereign, nominally the Queen of Australia, has been represented by a Viceroy, usually Australian-born. But the present Prime Minister, Mr Paul Keating, is advocating that Australia, like Fiji and South Africa, become a Republic. This is most likely to happen on 1 January 2001, one hundred years after Australia became a member of the Commonwealth. By the system Nostradamus predicts, it seems that it will be a presidential type, where the president choses his ministers wherever he likes, not necessarily from Parliament. It is quite common for children to be born with teeth. However, it could mean that that child will have the 'gift of the gab'.

After World War Two, three royal sons will be the ruin of Great Britain.

> *Aufin du Var changer le Pompotans;*
> *Pres du rivage, le trois beaux enfans naitre.*
> *Ruine ay peuple par age competans.*
> *Regne ay pays changer plus voir croistre.*
>
> VIII:97

At the end of the War, the (all powerful nation) will change.
Near the riverbank, the three beautiful infants will be born
Ruin of the people when they are of age
The realm and nation will alter by much growth.

There is a river Var in France, flowing between Cannes and Nice, but I believe it is an anagram for 'war' for then it would fit correctly. 'The riverbank' is that of the Thames, where Elizabeth II gave birth to three sons and a daughter after World War Two. Many believe that the Princess Royal is the only capable one of the four. Prince Charles has lurched from one blunder to another. Andrew, Duke of York's marriage grows hot and cold, while Prince Edward, in giving up a military career, shocked the nation. The first true monarch was William I, the last will be William V, the elder of Prince Charles's sons.

Charles, Prince of Wales, will have his heart from heaven.

Un prince Anglais Mars a son coeur de ciel
  Voudre pour suivre sa fortune prospere;
Des deux duelles l'un percera le fiel,
  Hai de lui, bien aimé de sa mere.

III:16

The English prince Mars has his heart from Heaven,
  He will wish to follow his prosperous fortune,
Of two duels, one will pierce his gall;
  Hated by him, well loved by his mother.

This is an ominous quatrain. As we learn from verse III:57, this is the last dynastical house. Charles, Prince of Wales, was born on 14 November 1948 in the Zodiacal house of Mars. He is known to be interested in the occult and spiritualism. He also desires to play a social part in the lives of his people to the annoyance of the politicians and public servants, instead of being a mere titular prince. In a sense, the rough way in which his favourite sport, polo, is played could be said to be a form of duelling. Several years ago while playing, his arm was painfully injured, requiring a stainless steel brace to be fitted. Now he has admitted adultery with Mrs Camilla Parker-Bowles and her husband has got a divorce; is he the one 'hated by him'? 'Well loved by his mother' would be natural. As all this is in the present, perhaps the whole story is yet to unfold.

Princess Diana will be enraged at her husband's adultery.

Dame en fureur par rage d'adultere,
  Viendra à son Prince conjurer non de dire;
Mais bref cogneu sera le vitupere,
  Que seront mis dix sept à martyre.

VI:59

The Lady furiously enraged at the adultery
  Shall conspire with her Prince to say nothing

But soon, the abuse becoming known,
  It will make the seventeen seem martyrs.

An accurate prophecy of the admitted adultery by Prince Charles that caused the ruin of his marriage and that of the co-respondent. 'The seventeen' in the last line are the Queen and her immediate royal family members, who are unable to intervene so, are innocent victims, or 'martyrs'.

A great earthquake at Cornwall will cause south-western Britain to sink.

Le tremblement de terre à Motara,
  Cassich saint George à demi perfondrez,
Paix asoupie, la guerre esveillera,
  Dans temple à Pasques abismes enfondrez.
                                             IX:31

A great trembling of the earth at Mortara,
  At Cassich. St George half sunk
Peace drowsy, war will escalate;
  In the Temple at Easter an abyss will open up.

A strange quatrain. The only Motara known is near Milan in Italy. One interpreter believes a misprint has taken place in the last letter, so he makes the word 'Mortars', which makes it more possible. 'Cassich', or tin island, is Cornwall. 'St George' stands for England. The hole in the temple or church floor could be due to earthquake or enemy action. Cornwall is mostly made of granite, so it is normally earthquake prone.

Great Britain will be ruled by American governor when Scotland is ice-bound

Le chef de Londres par regne l'Americh,
  L'isle de L'Escosse tempiera par gellee;

Roi Reb auront un si faux antechrist
  Que les mettra trestous dans la meslee.
                                    X:66

The chief of London by American rule,
  Will pave the Scotch isle with frost;
King Reb will be a false Antichrist,
  Who will put all into a melee.

There has been much speculation as to what this quatrain is
predicting. This is the verse which made some people object to the
American atomic-powered Polaris submarines being based on the
Clyde, 'Cold things in Scotland'. It appears that Great Britain will
secede from the Common Market and become a minor country.
Things will deteriorate further and the Americans will make her a
colony under a stern governor that will earn him the title of the 'Red
King', red being an anagram of 'Reb'. It seems from the last line that
anarchy will be rife at that time in England.

**Important British and German dignitaries captured by eastern
seamen.**

Le chef d'Escosse avec six d'Alemaigne,
  Par gens de mer Orienteaux captif;
Traverseront le Calpre et Espaigne,
  Present en Perse au nouveau Roy craintif.
                                    III:78

The Chief of Scotland with six Germans
  By Oriental seamen will be taken captive
Passing Gibraltar and Spain
  He will be presented in Iran to the new dreadful King.

This could be a very imminent event. The Scotch 'chief' could be any
member of the royal family; Prince Philip is the 'Duke of Edinburgh'.
These seamen are obviously terrorists and the abduction could take
place anywhere. To Nostradamus, 'Scotland' could mean Great

Britain, so a cabinet minister could be the victim. The Anglican Bishop of Edinburgh, primate of Scotland, whose comments about adultery have been reported by the media worldwide, could also be the predicted 'chief of Scotland'. As the son of the Duke of Edinburgh, the Prince of Wales could qualify to be the 'chief of Scotland'. Every time he leaves Great Britain on a pleasure or goodwill tour, he runs the risk of making this quatrain a prophecy.

3

MODERN TIMES AND INVENTIONS

World War Two is over. A long peace. People will travel by air, land, sea and hovercraft.

> *Les fleaux passés, diminue le monde,*
> *Long temps la paix, terres inhabitées;*
> *Seur marchera par ciel, terre, mer et onde;*
> *Puis de nouveau les guerres suscitées.*
>
> I:63

The scourges past, the world smaller
   Peace for a long time, lands inhabited
All shall travel safely by air, land, sea and wave,
   Then again the wars will reoccur.

The 50 years since the end of World War Two have been the golden age for everyone all over the world. At no other age have the ordinary people been able to enjoy the fruits of civilisation like these last few years. They have also experienced better food, health, clothing, accommodation and transport to see the rest of the world. But now the seeds of disintegration are sprouting up again, with wars in every part of the globe. Note, our seer foresaw air travel, an impossibility in his day but, more amazingly, be saw the hovercraft and the hydrofoil when he wrote about travelling on the 'onde', or wave, for literally that is what both types do.

Old roads will be improved and the Suez Canal a new route to Egypt.

> *Les vieux chemins seront tous embellis*
> *L'on passera à Memphis somentree*
> *Le grand Mercure d'Hercules fleur de lis*
> *Faisant trembler terre, mer et contree.*
> X:79

The old roads will be all improved
  There will be a similar passage to Memphis.
The grand Mercury d'Hercules is the Fleur de Lys
  Making the land, sea and country shake.

In the period since the last great war, worldwide the roads have been vastly improved; sea transport has also undergone vast improvement. The 'fleur de lys' (France) built the Suez Canal, a task fit for the 'great Mercury of Hercules.' About the last line, anyone living near a motor highway will tell one how when traffic goes by, the land or countryside trembles and shakes.

Settlers will go to the New World to populate vacant land.

> *Nouveau venus lieu basti sans defence.*
> *Occuper la place par lors inhabitable*
> *Pres maisons, champs, villes prendre à plaisance,*
> *Faim, peste, guerre, arpens long labourable.*
> II:19

Newcomers will build a place without defence,
  To occupy a place not then inhabited
Then in houses, fields, villages, they will take pleasure;
  Famine, plague, war, acres will long be workable.

This prophecy describes the settling of the two Americas and Australia and New Zealand by immigrants from Europe. At first I without fortifications between neighbours, they cleared the land by dint of hard labour. Then came famine, pests, finally war. Then, as a result of research, they are making the land more productive than ever.

When the French built the Suez Canal and lost its control, they made it an asset to Islam.

> *Par la discorde negligence Gauloise*
> *Sera passage à Mahomm et ouvert;*
> I:18

> By the discord and French negligence
> A passage shall be open to Mahomet;

The French built the Suez Canal and in the 1956 Suez Crisis President Nasser took it by nationalising it. It is now of the utmost importance to Islam (Mahomet) for Muslim fleets, armies and commerce and is of great importance in unifying Moslem countries.

A prophecy of hot air balloons 140 years before their invention.

> *Istra du Mont Gaulfier et Aventin,*
> *Qui par trou avertira l'armée;*
> V:57

> Out from Mont Gaulfier and Aventine
> Who, by the hole, will warn the army;

Note the words 'Mont Gaulfier'. The Montgolfier brothers invented the hot-air balloon and it was first used in warfare at the 1794 Battle of Fleurus, when it warned French troops of the enemy's movements, which were observed from above.

The skyscrapers and city canyons predicted.

> *Jardin du monde aupres de cité neufue*
> *Dans le chemin des montaignes cavees;*
> X:49

The Garden of the World near the new city
In the road of the hollow mountains;

In this foreseen portrait of modern New York, our seer wrote of
skyscrapers. One commentator called them 'man-made mountains';
another calls them the 'tunnelled mountains'.

A city on a plain covered with glass houses.

> *Le grand cité d'ocean maritime*
> *Environnee de marets en crystal.*
> IX:48

The great maritime city of the ocean
With an environment of crystal;

Here we have something common to many modern cities. Our seer is
describing a city surrounded by glass or greenhouses. In his day glass
was expensive and its use, carried a high rate of tax, so only the
wealthy could afford to own them.

**Samarobryn shall fly around the Earth free of politicians and their
laws.**

> *Si grand famine par une pastifere.*
> *Par pluie longue le long du pole Artique.*
> *Samarobryn cent lieux de l'hemisphere,*
> *Vivront sans loi exempt de politique.*
> VI:5

So great a famine by a plague
  By a long rain along the Arctic Pole.
Samarobryn a hundred leagues from the hemisphere,
  Living without law, exempt from politics.

There are two prophecies in this quatrain. The first two lines describe the fallout from the 1986 Chernobyl disaster, which went around the north pole destroying vegetation and thousands of lives. Even today people are dying from the cancer it caused.

The last two lines are about an astronaut living in a spacecraft which is circumnavigating the earth at the height of some 276 miles up. The meaning of 'Samarobryn' is still a mystery. In my previous book, I came up with 'flying robin', because I could see part of a 'robin' as in an anagram. In Mr P. Lemesurier's recent book, *Nostradamus: the next 50 years*, he believes the word is made up of two Russian ones 'samo' (self) and 'robotnik' (worker). This may be true, for Nostradamus took words from all sources besides creating some of his own. The Russian astronaut, Yuri Gagarin (1934–68) was the first man to fly around planet Earth, at the height of 301 km, or 187 miles, and while he was in space he was 'exempt from politics'.

When man landed on the Moon, he landed on a strange land.

Dedans le coing de Luna viendra rendre,
  Ou sera prins et mis en terre estrange,
Les fruitz immeurs seront à la grand esclandre
  Grand vitupere, à l'un grand louange.

IX:65

He will come to take himself to the corner of the Moon,
  Where he will be taken and placed on a strange land.
The immature fruit will be a great scandal,
  Great abuse to one, to the other great praise.

A wonderful prediction of the Russo-American race to put the first man on the Moon. The first two lines describe the astronaut's impressions on landing on the Moon while the other two foresee the disappointment of the Russians at having lost the race and the jubilation of the American people that their men had won.

The planet Neptune described 300 years before its discovery.

Jupiter joinct plus Venus qu'à la Lune,
  Apparoissant de plenitude blanche;
Venus cachée souz la blancheur Neptune
  De Mars frappée par la gravée branche.

IV:33

Jupiter joined more to Venus than the Moon
  Appearing in its fullness whitish.
Venus hidden under Neptune's whiteness,
  Mars struck by the engraved branch.

In this occult quatrain, the planet Venus is stated to be eclipsing the planet Neptune, which was not discovered by astronomers until the middle of the 19th century. It was 45 years after Nostradamus's death that Galileo used the first practical telescope to discover the wonders of the solar system.

The study of the universe will reduce the wonders of God.

Corps sublimes sans fin à l'oeil visibles;
  Obnubiler viendront par ses raisons
Corps, front comprins, sens chief et invisibles.
  Diminuant les sacrées oraisons.

IV:25

Endless heavenly bodies shall be seen by eye
  To come to cloud the senses
The body, with forehead, senses and head will be invisible.
  Making the sacred prayers diminish.

Telescopes were yet to be invented in Nostradamus's day; he here predicted that the future study of astronomy will belittle the wonders of God, making the people agnostics.

The electricity that will talk will need great care.

> *Quand l'animal à l'homme domestique,*
> *Apres grand peines et sauts viendra parler,*
> *De foudre à vierge sera si malefique,*
> *De terre prinse et suspendre en l'air.*
>
> III:44

When the animal tamed by man
   After great difficulty and advances shall come to talk
The lightning to the rod so bad
   That it must be taken from the earth and held in the air.

A wonderful foresight of electricity that powers machines and shows pictures while talking. Our seer apparently knew of the lengthy processes in its evolution and the great care that has to be taken when handling electricity.

The submarine with its periscope will scour the seas like a greedy god.

> *D'où pensera faire venir famine,*
> *De là viendra le rassassiement;*
> *L'oeil de la mer par avare canine*
> *Pour de l'un, l'autre donra huile, froment.*
>
> IV:15

From where one thought would make famine come
   From there will come plenty;
The eye of the sea like a greedy dog
   For the one, the other oil and wheat.

Here we have the submarine blockade of both World Wars. 'The eye of the sea' was the submarine's periscope, unheard of in the time of

Nostradamus. The first two lines state the fact that despite the great loss by submarines of ships by Great Britain, by severe rationing Great Britain had a greater supply of goods than did Europe, where there was dire starvation.

Carrying war plans, General Mark Clark lands by submarine in Africa.

Quand dans poisson fer et lettres enfermée,
  Hors sortira qui puis fera la guerre;
Aura par mer sa classe bien ramée,
  Apparoissant pres le Latine terre.

II:5

When in an iron fish with letters enclosed
  He shall then go out to make war.
He shall have on the sea his fleet well provided,
  To appear near the Latin land.

This is the historic exploit of the American General Mark Clark, when he landed from a submarine with plans and instructions for the American landing in Morocco in October 1942. Morocco was then French, or 'Latin', territory.

Allied amphibious tanks and DUKWS land on the Normandy beaches on D-Day, 1944.

Quand la poisson terrestre et aquatique,
  Par forte vague au gravier sera mis; □
Sa forme estrange sauve et horrifique,
  Par mer aux murs bien tost les ennemis.

I:29

When the terrestrial and aquatic fish,
  By a strong wave shall be cast upon the gravel
Its form strange, smooth, and horrible,
  By sea to the walls, will soon be the enemies.

An accurately predicted account of the landing of amphibious tanks in Normandy to assault Hitler's 'Fortress Europe'.

If the finder of Tutankhamen's tomb does not close it again, evil will befall him.

Qui ouvrira le monument trouvé
Et ne viendra le serrer promptement,
Mal lui viendra et ne pourra prouvé,
Si mieux doit estre Roi, Breton ou Normand.

IX:7

Whoever opens the discovered monument
And does not close it again promptly
Evil shall come to him. He will not be able to prove
Which King is better, a Breton or Norman.

After many years of searching, the English archaeologist Howard Carter in 1922 discovered the ancient Pharaonic tomb of Tutankhamen. An inscription over the tomb's entrance promised death to all who entered. Over a period of years all those who had been associated in the tomb's discovery died in various mysterious circumstance.

AIDS will plague the world, there will be relief but no cure.

Pau, Verone, Vicense, Sarragouse.
De glaives loings terroirs le sang humides,
Peste si grande viendra à la grand gousse,
Proche secours, et bien loing les remedes.

III:75

Pau, Verona, Vicenze, Saragossa.
Swords moist with blood from distant lands
A plague so great, will come with big scabs
Relief will be near and cure far away.

The cities in the first line are in France, Italy and Spain, implying that AIDS will be international. 'Knives' or 'swords' in tarotry stand for the phallus, or penis. If that is accepted then the verse's meaning becomes clear for, as is common knowledge, there is relief for AIDS but a remedy is yet to be found. The word 'gouse' or scab makes a doubt for this prophecy, for only in some AIDS cases are there scabs. Perhaps Nostradamus had syphilis in mind when he wrote this verse. It is believed that in his time syphilis was reaching Europe from the New World and that then there was no cure for it.

4

HISTORICAL PEOPLE

Comte de la Perouse killed by natives at Vanikoro, New Hebrides.

La nef estrange par le tourment marin,
  Abourdera pres de port incogneu;
Nonobstant signes de rameau palmerin,
  Apres mort pille avis tard venu.

I:30

The strange ship shall be tormented at sea,
  Approaching near an unknown port.
Notwithstanding the signs of palm branches,
  Then death and pillage, good advice comes late.

This verse could fit the fate of many explorers of the age of discovery. One reviewer says this is Ponce de Leon, the discoverer of Florida, who was killed by Indians in Cuba. Then it could be Ferdinand Magellan, who died in the Moluccas on his epic voyage around the world in 1520. As these events occurred before our prophet's death, and knowing how patriotic he was, I have chosen the Comte de la Perouse, a French explorer whose ship was wrecked at Vanikoro, New Hebrides, now known as Vanuatu, in 1789.

The South Pacific has the location and climate opposite to Babylon.

Soubs l'opposite climat Babylonique
Grand sera de sang effusion;
Que terre et mer, air, ciel sera inique,
Secte, faim, regnes, pestes, confusion.

I:55

In the lands with an opposite climate to Babylon
   There shall be so great an effusion of blood
That Heaven will seem unjust on land, sea and air,
   Sects, hunger, realms, plagues – all in confusion.

The antipodes to Babylon is 33–22 south and 155 west, a vacant area midway between New Zealand and Pitcairn Island. No doubt Nostradamus was trying to name what we call today the South Pacific. In my previous book I attributed this verse to Fletcher Christian and his *Bounty* mutineers but I now realise the verse belongs to the present. The former European powers divided these South Pacific isles among themselves. But recent circumstances have impoverished them, now finding colonies more liabilities than assets. France is the only nation still holding colonies in this area. All the rest are now miniature, independent, over-populated states, strapped for cash and threatened by rising sea levels which could make some disappear. France has recently put down a bid for independence from its native Kanaka population in New Caledonia. A truce has been declared and, after a referendum, the issue will be decided in 1998. In Papua New Guinea a civil war has been raging for some years now because inhabitants of copper-rich Bougainville Island want independence. In New Zealand the one-in-seven Maori population want their own courts because some of their ancestors did not sign the Treaty of Waitangi. One of the tiny states, Tonga (or Friendly Islands) is a Kingdom with its own native King. In Fiji, a Republic was declared in 1987 and it is no longer part of the British Commonwealth.

The freebooter Pizarro robs the Inca temples of their gold.

> *Mis tresor temple citadins Hesperiques*
> *Dans icelui retiré en secret lieu,*
> *Le temple ouvrir les liens fameliques,*
> *Reprens, ravis proie horrible au milieu.*
>
> X:81

Treasure will be placed in a temple by Hesperian citizens
Then withdrawn to a secret place;
The temple will be opened for bands of hungry ones,
Retaken, ravished, horrible prey in the midst.

This quatrain explains the deeds of Pizarro and his conquistadores who were never satisfied with their loot from the Incas, the western or 'Hesperian citizens'. Gold to the Incas had no commercial value, only as offerings to their gods, so was held in common in their temples. When the Spaniards came, the gold was removed to beyond their reach, hence the second line, but some was used to ransom their Emperor Atahualpa – but in vain, for they still put him to death.

Chairman Mao led his people on the 'long march' and they believed him to be God.

> *Loin hors du regne mis en hazard voyage*
> *Grand host duira pour soi l'occupera,*
> *Le Roi tiendra les siens captif ostage*
> *A son retour tout pays pillera.*
>
> VIII:92

Far distant from the realm, taken on hazardous voyage
He will lead a great host which he will make his own,
The King will hold his people captive as hostages
On his return he will pillage the whole country.

This verse could be applied to Hernando Cortez and his conquest of

Mexico, but I think it is better applied to Mao Tse-Tung who, to escape the Japanese, led his people on the Long March. This was a journey on foot of some thousands of miles over snowy mountains. On his return, he established the People's Republic of China and after writing his 'little red book' he was revered and treated like a God.

Catherine the Great vexed all Europe and the World.

> *Vers Aquilon grands efforts par Hommasse*
> *Presque l'Europe et l'univers vexer,*
> *Les deux eclipses mettre en telle chasse,*
> *Et aux Pannons vie et mort renforcer.*
>
> VIII:15

Towards the North great efforts by a masculine woman
    Almost all Europe and the world she will vex.
The two eclipses shall be put to flight,
    And to the Hungarians, life and death strengthened.

Catherine the Great (1729–96) of Russia is foretold here. 'The two eclipses' were her victories over the Turks in 1792 and the partition of Poland. The 'reinforcement of Hungary' was their share of the partition of Poland.

King Charles Emmanuel of Sardinia reigned only three years.

> *Dans la Sardaigne un noble Roi viendra*
> *Qui ne tiendra que trois ans le royaume,*
> *Plusieurs couleurs avec soi conjoindra,*
> *Lui mesme apres soin someil marrit scome.*
>
> VIII:88

Into Sardinia will come a noble king
    Who will hold the kingdom only three years.
He will join many colours to his own;
    He, after taunts, cares, spoils, will slumber.

Charles Emmanuel IV of Sardinia resigned his Italian estates to the French in 1798. He then reigned in Sardinia for three years before abdicating in favour of his brother. He then lived in a monastery in Rome, a broken man.

The mad monk, Rasputin, shall have a strange doctrine.

Par fureur faincte d'esmotion divine,
  Sera la femme du grand fort violee;
Juges voulants damner telle doctrine,
  Victime au peuple ignorant immolee.
                                    VI:72

By a feigned fury of divine emotion
  Will the wife of the great one be violated;
The judges will wish to damn such a doctrine
  As a victim of ignorant people he will be sacrificed.

The weird monk, Rasputin (1872–1916), by faith healing kept the boy Czarevitch alive for five years. Critics claimed during this time he was the Czarina's lover (lines one and two). Naturally, court officials discreetly found fault (line three). His great strength made him difficult to murder, but eventually a city mob threw his body into the River Neva to drown, the meaning of the last line.

The free city of Orange will be enslaved by harbouring undesirables.

La cité franche de liberté fait serve,
  Des profligés et reseurs faict asile;
Le Roy changé à eux non si proterve
  De cent seront devenus plus de mille.
                                    IV:16

The free city of liberty shall become an enclave,
  Of the profligates and dreamers, it will become an asylum
    which
The king will change, to them will not be so protective.
  From a hundred they will become a thousand.

In the middle ages Europe had many free cities where discontents
could live in peace. One such was Orange, close to where our seer
lived. In 1713 Orange became part of France, where no doubt Louis
XIV was 'not so protective' to these undesirables.

**The nine judges of the USA Supreme Court will make separate
verdicts.**

D'humain troupeau neuf seront mis à part,
  De jugement et conseil separez;
Leur sort sera divise en depart,
  Kappa, Theta, Lambda, mort bannis esgarez.
                                              I:81

Of the human flock, nine shall be set apart,
  Separate in judgment and counsel
Their destiny is to be divided as they go.
  Kappa, Theta, Lambda, dead, banished, scattered.

The 'nine' are the chief justices of the United States Supreme Court
who, on serious cases, each bring down their own verdict. The case is
decided by the greatest number in favour. In the last line the letters
are 'K', 'TH', and 'L' of the ancient Greek alphabet. The meaning of
the last line is, all learning will be forgotten; the case to be decided on
human justice or its own merits.

Abraham Lincoln shall raise the humble and vex the slave owners.

La sacree pompe viendra baisser les ailes,
  Par la venue du grand legislateur;

Humble haussera vexera les rebelles,
  Naistra sur terre aucun aemulateur.
                    V:79

The sacred pomp will come to lower the wings
  For the coming of the Great Legislator.
He will raise the humble, vex the rebels,
  No emulator will ever be born on Earth.

President Abraham Lincoln is nicely foretold in this quatrain; the humble lawgiver and president. In the third line his opposition to the break-away Southern States, 'the rebels', is predicted. .

F. D. Roosevelt will pray on Thursday and be a menace to the Japanese.

De l'aquatique triplicité naistra
  D'un qui fera le jeudi pour sa feste;
Son bruit, loz, regne, sa puissance croistra,
  Par terre et mer aux Oriens tempeste.
                    I:50

Of the aquatic triplicity will be born
  One who will make Thursday his festival;
His fame, praise, rule and power shall grow
  By land and sea, to become to Orientals a tempest.

President F. D. Roosevelt is prophesied here. 'Thursday as a festival' is a reference to the American custom of celebrating the fourth Thursday in November as Thanksgiving Day. The last line refers to the defeats suffered by the Japanese, inflicted by the American forces of President Roosevelt in World War Two.

President Roosevelt, though he came late, was the one needed.

Sur le milieu du grand monde la rose,
  Pour nouveaux faict sang public espandu;
A dire vrai on aura bouche close,
  Lors au besoing viendra tard l'attendu.
                                                V:96

Out of the middle of the world will be the rose
  For new deeds public blood will be spilt
To tell the truth everyone shall close the mouth,
  Then though he come late, the one awaited.

The longest serving US President, F. D. Roosevelt, is predicted here.
Line one is a pun on his name. 'Welt' in German means world. With
'rose' and 'welt' we get Roosevelt. The last line is a take-off at his
country's late entry into World War Two, when the Americans were
desperately 'awaited' by their allies in Europe.

**Seers predicted that the Kennedy brothers would die: one by day,
the other at night.**

Le grand du foudre tumbe d'heure diurne,
  Mal et predict par porteur postulaire;
Suivant presage tumbe d'heure nocturne,
  Conflict Reims, Londres, Etrusque pestifere.
                                                I:26

The great one will be struck down by lightning by day
  The evil predicted by the bearer of a petition.
According to the prophecy another falls at night-time.
  A conflict between Rheims and London. A plague in
  Tuscany.

Numerous clairvoyants predicted the tragic death of both Kennedy
Brothers, saying one at mid-day and the other at midnight, exactly as
did happen. The conflict between Rheims (France) and London

(Great Britain) was president De Gaulle's opposition to Great Britain joining the European Common Market.

When President Kennedy dies, an older man will rule.

La mort subite du premier personnage,
  Aura changé et mis un autre au regne;
Tost, tard venu à si haut et bas aage,
  Que terre et mer faudre que on la craigne.

IV:14

The sudden death of the chief personage
  Will make a change and put another to rule.
Late to come so high a degree and so low an age,
  That by land and sea there will be need to fear him.

An interesting prophecy concerning President J. F. Kennedy. His sudden death brought L. B. Johnson to be sworn in as President almost immediately. The third line is astonishing; one so low an age to so high a position, now to one of so high an age, all of which was true. The last line is a reference to the Cuban missile confrontation with Nikita Khrushchev which threatened a World War until the Russians backed off.

A Pope will reign for 17 years, then five will follow in that time.

Apres le siege tenu dix sept ans,
  Cinq changeront en tel revolu terme;
Puis sera l'un esleu de mesme temps,
  Qui des Romains ne sera trop conforme.

V:92

After the see (Vatican) has been held for 17 years
  Five changes will take place in that period of time;
Then one will be elected at that time,
  Who to the Romans will not be very conformable.

Pope Pius XII reigned for 19 years; John XXIII from 1958 to 1963, five years; Pope Paul from 1963 to 1978, 15 years; Pope John-Paul I thirty days in 1978. The same year, Pope John-Paul II was elected. So in twenty years from 1958 to 1978 there were five different Popes in Rome. If this is accepted, Pope John-Paul II would fulfil the last two lines because he is the only non-Italian Pope since 1522 – a period of 452 years – a fact that would not be very pleasing to the people of Rome, as Popes are usually Italian born.

Pope John XXIII will hold the papacy for four years. Paul VI will be less popular.

> *Quatre ans le siege quelque bien peu tiendra,*
> *Un surviendra libidineux de vie;*
> *Ravenne et Pise, Veronne soustiendront,*
> *Pour eslever la croix de Pape envie.*

VI:26

> For four years the seat will be held for a little good
> One will succeed of a libidinous life;
> Ravenna, Pisa and Verona will support him
> For elevating the Papal Cross to life.

Pope John XXIII reigned for just over four years. He was the common people's Pope, whereas Paul VI was more withdrawn and not so popular. The three cities named are in Italy, meaning that all Italy will support the Pope in propagating the faith. Before being elected Pope, he was the Cardinal of Venice, the see that included the cities named.

Pope John Paul I's abundance of goodness was the cause of his sudden death.

> *Esleu en Pape, d'esleu sera mocqué,*
> *Subit soudain esmeu prompt et timide,*

120

Par trop bon doulx à mourir provocqué,
  Crainte estainte la nuit de sa mort guide.
                              X:12

Elected as Pope, the elected will be mocked,
  His sudden removal, prompt and timid;
By too much sweetness he is provoked to die
  Fearing on the night of death for his guide.

After reigning only 30 days, Pope John Paul I died suddenly at night
amid suspicion. He was elected at a time when great financial
scandals afflicted the Vatican involving high Vatican dignitaries.
These affairs took place before he took office and he was investigat-
ing them when he suddenly died. The 'guide' in the last line would be
his accountant or financial expert who was assisting him in
unravelling the situation.

**Pope John Paul I will be elected the day after the tomb of St Peter is
found.**

Quand le sepulcre du grand Romain trouvé,
  Le jour apres sera esleu Pontife;
Du senat gueres il ne sera prouvé,
  Empoisonné son sang au sacré scyphe.
                              III:65

When the tomb of the great Roman is found,
  The next day, a pope will be elected;
Of whom the Senate will not approve,
  His blood poisoned in the Sacred Chalice.

In 1978, a tomb was discovered under St Peter's which is believed to
be that of St Peter, the Apostle. Although Popes are elected by a
meeting of cardinals, the Pope is assisted by the Curia (or Senate). It
is widely believed that John Paul was poisoned by a drink on retiring
on the night of his death.

Now that European empires are ended, so will Christianity slowly fade.

> Regne d'Eglise par mer succombera,
>> V:25

The rule of the Church of the sea shall succumb,

'The Church of the sea' is Christianity. When the European nations colonised most of the rest of the world, their missionaries converted many of the natives to Christianity. Now these former colonies are independent states, Christianity is declining. The task Christ set his disciples of dispersing the Gospel is over. Islam and the pre-European beliefs are taking over again.

Louis Pasteur, the French scientist, will be honoured as a god.

> Perdu trouvé, caché de si long siecle,
>> Sera Pasteur demi-Dieu honoré;
> Ains que la Lune acheve son grand siecle,
>> Par autres vents sera deshonoré.
>>> I:25

Lost, found, hidden for so many centuries
  Pasteur like a demi-god will be honoured;
This when the moon completes her great cycle.
  But by other minds shall be dishonoured.

Here is predicted the famous French scientist Louis Pasteur (1822–95), a pioneer of medicine who reintroduced ancient ideas. In the last line is foretold that many of his contemporaries will claim that he is a charlatan.

122

General Franco and the Spanish Civil War.

L'un des plus grands fuira aux Espaignes
Qu'en longue playe apres viendra saigner;
Passant copies par les hautes montaignes,
Devastant tout et puis paix regner.

III:54

One of the greatest men will flee into Spain
That will cause a wound to come to bleed long,
Armies will cross over high mountains
Devastating everything and then reign in peace.

General Francisco Franco (1892–1975) was exiled to the Canary
Isles as Governor and then flew back to start the Spanish Civil War,
which cost over 600,000 lives. The Italian and German volunteers
were those who crossed the 'high mountains'. Spain was neutral
during World War Two. The 'peace' lasted from 1939 until his death
in 1975.

The assassination of King Humberto of Italy, July 1900.

Le bras pendu et la jambe liée
Visage pasle au sein poignard caché;
Trois qui seront jurez de la meslee
Au grand de Gennes sera le fer lasché.

V:28

The arm hanging and leg bound
The face pale, a dagger hidden in the chest,
Three will be sworn to the mêlée,
To the great one Genoa will the knife be drawn.

King Humberto of Italy (Gennes is Italian for Genoa and stands for
Italy) was assassinated by a smith named Acciarito on 29 July 1900.

5

WORLD WARS ONE AND TWO

For the most part, Nostradamus treated World Wars One and Two as one conflict because the principal antagonists were the same, except that Japan and Italy changed sides and Spain and Turkey were neutral in the second war. I can find no reference to the Kaiser. Our seer's chief target was Adolf Hitler, whom he believed was an Anti-Christ, a founder of his own creed or religion. Hitler, when told of the references about him in the 'The Centuries', must have had second thoughts, for he certainly used them to further his propaganda to mislead his victims.

I will start with those dealing with World War One.

The French-born King Ferdinand deserted France to gain Macedonia and lost it all.

> *Et Ferdinand blonde sera descorte*
> *Quitter la fleur suivre le Macedon.*
> *Au grand besoin faillira sa routte,*
> *Et marchera contre le Myrmidon.*
> IX:35

And blond Ferdinand will be detached
A quitter of the Fleur(de Lys) to follow Macedonia.

In his great need his road will fail him,
And he will march against the Myrmidons.

Born a French prince, King Ferdinand of Bulgaria was expected to join the Western allies, but he sided with the central European Powers in the hope of being rewarded with Macedonia as his part in the spoils of victory. But when they lost, he lost his throne. The 'Flower' was the French 'Fleur de Lys'. 'Myrmidons' here means the majority.

The French people will be disturbed by alien soldiers billeting in their midst.

Tours, Orleans, Blois, Angiers, Reims et Nantes
Cités vexées par subit changement;
Par langues estranges seront tendues tentes,
Fleuves, dards Renes, terre et mer tremblement.

I:20

Tours, Orleans, Blois, Angers, Reims and Nantes
Cities vexed by sudden change,
By strange tongues tents will be erected,
Rivers, darts at Rennes, land and sea all shaking.

In World War One troops from all parts of the Earth camped in the French countryside to stop the German advance. This verse describes the French people's feelings and apprehensions. 'Darts' are long range shells which, when they landed and exploded, shook the countryside for miles around.

The French and British launch strong attacks on the Dardanelles in April 1915.

Vers Aquitaine par insuls Britanniques
De pars eux mesmes grands incursions
Pluies, gelees feront terroirs uniques,
Port Selyn fortes fera invasions.

II:1

126

Towards Aquitaine by British assaults
And by means of great invasions,
Rains, frosts, will make the terrain unsafe.
Port Selyn strong against invasions.

When the Allies were checked on the Western Front, an attempt was made to open another front by forcing a passage to the Black Sea. France (Aquitaine) and Great Britain attacked both sides of the entrance to the Dardanelles, in an attempt to take Istanbul (Port Selyn), then known as Constantinople. But because of abnormally bad weather, stout Turkish resistance and heavy losses, they had to evacuate the territory they had gained.

Battleships bombard Gallipoli until losses by mines become too great.

La legion dans la marine classe,
   Calcine, Magnes, soulphre et poix bruslera;
Le long repos de l'asseuree place,
   Port Selyn, chercher feu les consumera.

IV:23

The legion in the marine fleet;
   Calcium, magnesium, sulphur and pitch shall burn.
A long rest in a safe place
   Port Selyn will be sought but fire will consume them.

Before the landings on Gallipoli, a combined Franco-British battle fleet tried to force their way into the Sea of Marmara but heavy losses, owing to mines, caused the attempt to fail. The 'legion' was the troops carried aboard the ships. The mixtures in the second line will make up the explosives in gunpowder used by the battleships. The third line records the long wait at the island of Lesbos before action. The last line is the sinking of ships by mines in the narrows of the Dardanelles.

British forces land on the Gallipoli Peninsula.

Proche à descendre l'armee crucigere
 Sera guettez par les Ismaëlites;
De tous cottez batus par nef Raviere
 Prompt assaillis de dix galeres eslites.

IX:43

Close to land, the army of Crosses
 Shall be watched by the Ismaelites (Turks)
Beaten on all sides by the ship Impetuous
 Immediately assailed by ten elite warships.

The Turkish defenders of Gallipoli had plenty of warning that an attack was imminent as the 'Army of the Crosses' had spent some weeks at the island of Lesbos, a short distance away. The flags of the British, Australian and New Zealand forces all had the Union Jack on their flags, which is composed of four crosses upon their national flags, hence the 'army of the crosses'. 'The ship Impetuous' would be a cruiser, courageously firing at short range, while the ten elite warships were the mighty battleships shelling from a distance. They were the *Queen Elizabeth* (flagship), *Lord Nelson*, *Prince George*, *Albion*, *Swiftsure*, *Dublin*, *Goliath*, *Talbot*, *Minerva* and *Vengeance*.

**After World War One shall follow the great plague, or 'Flu'
epidemic.**

L'horrible guerre qu'en l'occident s'apreste
 L'an ensuivant viendra la pestilence,
Si fort horribles que jeune, vieux, ne beste,
 Sang, feu, Mercure, Mars, Jupiter en France.

IX:55

A horrible war will be prepared in the west,
 The year following, will come the pestilence;

So very horrible that neither young, old or beast shall escape,
  Blood, fire, Mercury, Mars, Jupiter, in France.

In the last months of 1918, returning soldiers from the war zones brought the germs of a plague back to their homelands with them. Although the virus died out quickly, while it lasted it is said that the number who died the sudden death from the plague, or 'Spanish Flu' equalled the number who had died from enemy action in the war.

The Maginot Line, built in 15 parts near the Rhine, was a failure.

Pres du grand fleuve, grand fosse, terre egeste
  En quinze pars sera l'eau divisee;
La cité prinse, feu, sang, cris conflict mettre
  Et la plus part concerne au collisee.

IV:80

Near a great river, a great earth ditch dug out,
  Into fifteen parts the water will be divided;
The city taken, fire, blood, cries, conflict set,
  And the great part concerned at the clash.

The infamous Maginot Line was created in fifteen parts just as Nostradamus predicted, between the years 1929-38 as a protection against Hitler's Germany. When the attack did come, it came north of the line through Belgium and Holland, so all its defenders were outflanked and useless. The last line expresses the French dismay at this result. I believe the Maginot Line will be very useful defending France from the north-east when fighting in Provence, in the coming assault from Muslim countries.

Seven days after the fall of the Maginot Line, the enemy will take Paris.

> *L'oiseau royal sur la cité solaire,*
> *Sept mois devant fera nocturne augure;*
> *Mur d'Orient cherra tonnerre esclaire,*
> *Sept jours aux portes les ennemis à l'heure.*
> V:81

The royal bird over the solar city
  For seven months ahead shall make nightly signs
The eastern wall shall fall, thunder will shine,
  In seven days the enemy will be at the gates.

Some attribute this verse to the wall built in Berlin post-war, but more likely it refers to the Maginot Line and the seven days, 5–11 June 1940, when the Germans swept through Belgium and Holland, by-passing the Maginot Line to take Paris. The first two lines would refer to a reconnaissance plane at high altitude making a survey of the battlefield.

Born of peasant stock, Mussolini will humble the aristocracy and take Italy's wealth.

> *Du mont royal naistra d'une casane,*
> *Qui duc, et compte viendra tyranniser*
> *Dresser copie de la marche Millane,*
> *Favene, Florence d'or et gens espuiser.*
> VII:32

Of Mont Reale will come one born in a cottage
  Who will tyrannise over duke and lord;
He will address the Milan army marchers,
  And exhaust Faenza and Florence of gold and men.

The seat of Italy's government is Mont Reale in Rome, from which

Mussolini was expelled at the closing years of the war. 'The March on Rome' began in Milan (1922) where he did address the marchers. For his military adventures he stripped Italy of wedding rings, brass cooking pans and anything of use for foreign currency.

Mussolini will play second fiddle to Hitler, who stole his ideas.

Romain pouvoir sera du tout abas,
  Son grand voisin imiter les vestiges;
Occultes haines civiles et debats,
  Retarderont aux bouffons leurs folies.
                                III:63

Roman power will be well abased.
  His great neighbour will imitate his steps;
Secret polite hatreds and debates
  Shall retard the follies of the buffoons.

Hitler exploited Mussolini's ideas of Fascism to his own advantage. To the outside world the antics of the two dictators, were amusing. The comedian Charles Chaplin made much of this in his successful film, *The Great Dictator*.

Mussolini will deny liberty to Italy, and signs the Concordat with the Pope.

La liberté ne sera recouvree,
  L'occupera noir fier vilain inique;
Quand la matiere du Pont sera ouvree,
  D'Hister, Venise faschée la Republique.
                                V:29

Liberty will be not recovered
  She will be occupied by a wicked, proud, black villain,
When the matter of the Pope is opened
  By Hitler, the Republic of Venice will be irate.

Mussolini and his Fascist party denied liberty to Italy. The signing of the Concordat (1929) with the Pope did not meet with Hitler's approval. 'The Republic of Venice' means Italy here, because the then king of Italy, Victor Emmanuel III, had no say in politics, so reigned only in name.

The Nazis will wear black shirts and burn books in the streets.

> *Apres les livres brusler les asiniers,*
> *Contraints seront changer habits divers;*
> *Les Saturnins brusler par les meusniers,*
> *Hors la plupart qui ne sera convers*
> VI:17

After the books will be burnt, the asses
  Will be forced to change into various clothes,
The Saturnines will be burnt by the millers
  Except the greater part who will not be found.

All books without official Nazi approval were burnt in city squares. Storm-trooper uniforms became everyday dress for men. The learned (Saturnines) were likely to be carried off to prison by the ignorant 'millers' so the intellectuals fled the country.

The French people will be divided about Hitler. Some for, others against.

> *L'oiseau de proie volant à la semestre,*
> *Avant conflict faict aux Francois pareure;*
> *L'un bon prendra l'un ambique sinistre,*
> *La partie foible tiendra par bon augure.*
> I:34

The bird of prey flying to the left
  Before the conflict with the French, will prepare:
One will assume good, the other bad,
  The weaker party will hold it as a good omen.

'The bird of prey' was Hitler, who 'flew' to the left looking at a map through Holland and Belgium. The French prepared the Maginot line on the right. There was much controversy in pre-war France about Hitler. Some were for him, others against. Hence the Vichy government, which co-operated with him.

Benito Mussolini, an undignified name, will be born in Northern Italy.

> *Le grand naistra de Veronne et Vincense*
> *Qui portera un surnon bien indigne.*
> *Qui a Venise vouldre faire vengeance.*
> *Lui mesme prins homme du guet et signe.*
> VIII:33

The great one will be born at Verona and Vincenza
  Who will have an undignified name
Who at Venice will try to take vengeance
  He, himself will be taken by a man of the watch and
    sign.

Benito Mussolini was born at Predappio, a short distance from both Verona and Vicenza, but in Northern Italy. His name means a 'Muslim worker'. At a conference held at Venice with Hitler, his grandiose ideas of a 'Mare Nostrum' were thwarted. The final line is a reference to his tragic fate when his dead body was strung up to a gallows in a Milan square by a mob.

Mussolini from nothing will advance quickly to govern Italy.

> *Dans peu dira faulse brute fragile,*
> *De bas en haut eslue promptement;*
> *Puis un instant desloyale et labile,*
> *Qui de Veronne aura gouverement.*
> I:12

In a little while a weak, false brute
  Will rise from low to high quickly,
Then in an instant disloyal and volatile
  Who at Verona shall have the government.

'Verona' here represents Italy. Another quatrain describing Mussolini's meteoric rise to power.

Mussolini's first prize is the king himself. He will be led astray by Hitler.

Premier grand fruit, le prince de Pesquiere
  Mais puis viendra bien et cruel malin,
Debans Venise perdra sa gloire fiere
  Et mis a mal par plus joune Celin.

VIII:31

His first great fruit will be the Prince of Pescheria
  But then he will become very cruel and malicious
In Venice he will lose his proud glory
  And is led into sin by a very young Turk.

Having been successful in the 1922 Fascist revolt, Mussolini's first prize was King Victor Emmanuel III himself. In 1917, after a crushing Italian defeat at Caperetto, the King had then assumed supreme command of his nation's forces at Pescheria, hence Nostradamus dubbed him 'Prince of Pescheria'. The third line refers to Mussolini's Venice meeting with Hitler, who would not grant him his wishes. Hitler is the 'young Turk' in the last line.

Hitler and 30 of his staff escape a bomb blast in a Munich cellar.

Peuple assemblé voir nouveau expectacle,
  Princes et Rois par plusiers assistans;
Pilliers faillir, murs, mais comme miracle
  Le Roi sauvé et trente des instants.

VI:51

People will assemble to see a new spectacle
    Princes and Kings with several assistants;
Pillars, walls will fall, but as a miracle
    The King saved and thirty others present.

This is the famous prediction of the attempt on Hitler's life in a
Munich beer cellar in November 1938. It was owing to Hitler's
premature departure that he and 30 others escaped. This was the
quatrain that Herr Ernst Krafft used to attract Hitler's attention that
Nostradamus had predicted the attempt, 380 years previously.

**The League of Nations will argue endlessly without making
decisions.**

Du Lac Leman les sermons fascheront,
    Les jours seront reduicts par sepmaines;
Puis mois, puis an, puis tous deffailliront,
    Les magistrats damneront leurs loix vaines.
                               I:47

At Lake Leman (Geneva) the speeches will be troublesome
    The days will be extended into weeks
Then months, then years, then be total failures;
    The magistrates will condemn their fruitless laws.

In November 1920 the League of Nations was set up in Geneva
(Lake Lemans) to settle differences between nations. But Germany,
Italy and Japan first of all argued strenuously, ignored any decisions
made, then finally resigned their membership because the League
had no power to enforce its deliberations. The first three lines
describe how these delaying tactics were used, making war inevitable.

The League of Nations proves a fruitless exercise.

Par les Sueves et lieux circonvoisins,
    Seront en guerre pour cause des nuees;

Gamp marins locustes et cousins,
  Du Leman fautes seront bien desnuees.
                                V:85

By Switzerland and surrounding places
  Will war because of the clouds,
Marine crabs, locusts and gnats;
  The faults of Geneva laid quite bare.

This quatrain is a ridicule of the meetings of the League of Nations, describing the paltry subjects they used to debate upon instead of the more serious subjects they should have been discussing.

Neville Chamberlain and the Munich pact. A dishonorable disgrace.

L'honnissement puant abominable
  Apres le faict sera felicité,
Grand excusé, pour n'estre favourable,
  Qu'à paix Neptune ne sera incité.
                                VI:90

The stinking and abominable shame
  Will be made nice, after the deed:
The great one excused for not being favourable,
  As for the peace, Neptune will not be excited.

In 1938, the Munich Past was signed by Prime Minister Neville Chamberlain, France and Adolf Hitler promising 'peace in our time'. But a year later Hitler made other demands on Poland, which he then invaded. 'Neptune' is Great Britain, then represented by Anthony Eden, who resigned over the pact. Then Mr Chamberlain resigned, to be succeeded by Winston Churchill.

Through Mussolini's folly the 'blue division' will be wiped out in the Crimea.

> *Peuple sans chef l'Espaigne et d'Italie,*
> *Morts, profligez dedans le Cherronesse;*
> *Leur dict trahi par legiere folie,*
> *Le sang nager tout à la traverse.*
>
> III:68

People of Spain and Italy without a leader
    Shall die, overcome in the Crimea;
Their dictator betrayed by stupid folly,
    The blood floating all around.

The Spanish had been supported by the Germans and Italians in the Spanish War so, as a gesture when Hitler attacked the Russians, the 'blue division' was raised, made up of Italians and Spaniards, which fought in the Crimean Peninsula, where it was wiped out to a man.

England and France will only ally due to necessity. Spain and Eire will remain neutral.

> *Terre Italique pres des monts tremblera,*
> *Lyon et coq non trop confederez;*
> *En lieu de peur, l'un l'autre s'aidera.*
> *Seul Castulon et Celtes moderez.*
>
> I:93

The Italian land near the Alps will be afraid;
    The Lion and the Cock will not confer well together
In place of fear, one will aid the other.
    Only Spain and Eire will be quite (neutral).

Communication between England (Lion) and France (Cock) has always been difficult. This was shown by the coolness in the War between the Free French leader, General de Gaulle, and Winston Churchill. 'Castulon' stands for Spain while the Irish are 'Celts'.

The *Bismark* sinks the *Hood*, then is crippled and sunk. Hitler is angry.

> *Navalle pugne nuit sera superee*
> *Le feu, naves à l'occident ruine,*
> *Rubriche neufve; le grand nef coloree;*
> *Ire à vaincu et victoire en bruine.*
>
> IX:100

> In a naval battle, night will be overcome
> By fire, ships of the West ruined,
> A new stratagem; The great ship coloured.
> Anger to the vanquished and victory in a fog.

In a few words, a perfect description of the sinkings of the *Bismark* and the *Hood*, one of the 'ships of the west'. England is to Germany's west. Then 'a new stratagem', the use of an aircraft carrier carrying six sea-planes, one of whose bombs damaged the *Bismark*'s steering gear. She was now trapped, moving in three mile circles. Small fast vessels were then brought up, lighting up the *Bismark* with their searchlights and making her a 'great ship coloured'. In the last line we have Hitler's annoyance at the loss of the pride of the German navy. Most of the action took place between Iceland and Greenland, where the Gulf Stream and Arctic waters meet, causing a continuous 'fog'.

General Freyberg V.C. escapes from Greece, defends Crete, then escapes again in a flying-boat.

> *Le chef qu'aura conduit peuple infiny,*
> *Loing de ciel, de meurs et langue estrange;*
> *Cinq mil en Crete et Thessalie fini,*
> *Le chef fuyant, sauvé en marine grange.*
>
> I:98

> The chief will lead an infinite people
> Far from their skies, to strange manners and tongues.

Five thousand in Crete, and Thessally finished;
    The chief fleeing, safe in a marine barn.

Mussolini annexed Albania in 1939. When he declared war on England and France in June 1940, he then invaded Greece but was repulsed, so a German army was sent to his aid. Immediately a British force from Egypt was sent to aid Greece. The 2nd New Zealand Division under General Freyberg was part of this force. The Germans proved too strong and drove the British and allies out of Greece from where they escaped to Crete, where Freyberg was made island-commander-in-chief. At the moment of his appointment he had only 5,000 men, although the numbers built up later. The 2nd NZ Division was an 'infinite people' because it was composed of the elite men from a small nation – its best educated, its best athletes etc. 'Far from the skies': it is impossible to get further from New Zealand than the Mediterranean Sea. 'To strange manners and tongues': at that time everyone in New Zealand spoke only English, but in the Mediterranean area people speak many tongues. General Freyberg escaped not in a fighter plane but in a slow-moving Sunderland flying-boat – literally a maid-of-all-work craft to carry stores etc, so it could be said to be 'a marine barn'.

Germans and Italians plunder Greece and the Aegean Sea islands.

La gent estrange divisera butins,
    Saturne en Mars son regard furieux;
Horrible estrange aux Tosquans et Latins,
    Grecs qui seront à frapper curieux.
                                        I:83

The strange people will divide the spoils,
    Saturn in Mars will show his furious look;
Strangely horrible to the Toscans and Latins
    The Greeks will make a curious strike.

In 1940, the Italians attacked Greece and her Aegean Sea islands and

139

after initial reverses the Germans came to their assistance. Much plunder was taken away. Lines two and three mean: to young soldiers new to battle, war plays strange tricks, so pillaging takes place. The last line means the Greeks became guerrillas.

Born of poor parents in Western Europe, Hitler will speak well and be famous in Japan.

> *Du plus profond de l'Occident d'Europe*
>   *De pauvres gens un jeune naistra;*
> *Qui par sa langue seduira grande troupe,*
>   *Son bruit au regne d'Orient plus croistra.*
>
> III:35

> In the deepest part of Europe
>   Of poor people shall an infant be born
> Who by his tongue shall seduce great crowds
>   His fame in the Eastern realm will grow even greater.

A very good description of Adolf Hitler, even as to his reputation among his eastern allies, the Japanese.

Hitler will unite the small states into an empire. Stalin will ruin him.

> *Translatera en la grand Germanie*
>   *Brabant et Flandres, Gand, Bruges et Bologne;*
> *La traifue fainte, le grand Duc d'Armenie*
>   *Assaillera Vienne et la Coloigne.*
>
> V:94

> He will change into Greater Germany
>   Brabant, Flanders, Ghent, Bruges and Boulogne;
> The truce feigned, The Great Duke of Armenia
>   Shall assault Vienna and Cologne.

'Greater Germany' was the Third Reich, created by Hitler. 'The

Grand Duke of Armenia' was Josef Stalin, who was born in neighbouring Georgia and who later did assault Vienna and Cologne in the final stages of the War. 'The false truce' occurred at the start of World War Two when Hitler and Stalin divided Poland and the Baltic states between them.

A man of the people, Hitler was born in Austria. No one will know where he went.

> *Aupres du Rhin des montaignes Noriques,*
>   *Naistra un grand de gens trop tard venu.*
> *Qui defendra Saurome et Pannoniques,*
>   *Qu'on ne scaura qu'il sera devenu.*
>   III:58

Near the Rhine in the Norican Mountains
    Shall be born a great one of the people, come too late
Who shall defend Poland and the Hungarians.
    It will never be known what became of him.

Hitler was born in 'Norica' near the Rhine and in Austria. When the Germans retreated, it could be said he was defending Poland and the Hungarians. At the end of the war, for a while there was some doubt as to his fate.

The man from Texas, General Eisenhower, will ruin the man from the Norican Mountains.

> *Premier en Gaule, premier en Romanie,*
>   *Par mer et terre aux Anglois et Paris;*
> *Merveilleux faitz par celle grand mesnie,*
>   *Violent Terax perdra le Norlaris.*
>   VIII:60

The first in France, the first in Romania,
    By sea and land to the English and Paris;

Marvellous feats by that grand company.
Violent Texas will ruin the Norlaris.

The first three lines predict Hitler's and the German army's exploits very well. In the last line, 'Terax' is an anagram for 'Texas', where General Eisenhower was born in Fort Denison in 1890. 'Norlaris' is an anagram for Lorraine, held by Hitler for the Third Reich.

Hitler, Mussolini and Japan sign the Tripartite Pact at the Brenner Pass.

> *En lieu bien proche non esloigné de Venus,*
> *Les deux plus grans de l'Asie et d'Affrique*
> *Du Rhin et Hister qu'on dira sont venus*
> *Cris, pleurs à Malte et costé Ligustique.*
>
> IV:68

At a nearby place not far from Venice
    The two great ones of Asia and Africa
Will say they are from the Rhine and Hister
    Cries, tears at Malta and the Ligurian coast.

This quatrain predicts the signing of the Tripartite Pact. Here the word 'Venus' stands for Venice. Not far away in the Alps is the Brenner Pass, where the two dictators met to sign with Japan, 'the great one of Asia'. Because of his then African possessions, Mussolini is the 'one of Africa'. 'Hister', an ancient name for the River Danube, here stands for Hitler. The result was a blockade of Malta and retaliatory air raids on Genoa.

84-year-old Marshal Pétain elected to rule France.

> *La grand pesche viendra plaindre pleurer,*
> *D'avoir esleu, trompés seront en l'aage;*

Guiere avec eux ne voudra demourer,
Deceu sera par ceux de son langaige.
VII:35

The great fish will come to wail and moan,
    Once elected, deceived by his age
He will not wish to stay long with them
    Being deceived by those of his own language.

Marshal Henri Pétain (1856–1951), a famous hero of the First World War, was elected to rule France, when it was about to be defeated. After the defeat Pétain was allowed to rule a third of France known as the Vichy Government. Powerless, he was only a puppet to Hitler, hence the first line 'he was only a great fish on a line, could only moan'. He was deceived by his lieutenant, Pierre Laval, who after the war was tried and executed for treason.

Pétain, the ruler of France, will be in senile decline and his country divided.

D'un chef viellard naistra sens hebeté,
    Degenerant par savoir et par armes;
Le chef de France par sa soeur redouté
    Champ divisez, concedez aux gendarmes.
I:78

To the old chief will be born one without sense
    Who shall degenerate in learning and arms;
The head of France will be feared by his sister
    Fields divided, conceded to the men of arms.

Being in his eighties, Marshall Pétain would have what is now called Alzheimer's Disease, where the patient increasingly loses his memory. This would account for his loss of learning and military tactics and his tyranny in the last line. It is reported that his sister, who lived in the USA, said he was unfit to rule. The last line would be that the country would be under martial law.

143

For 20 months Pétain will rule France to be followed by one even worse.

> *Le vieux frustré du principal espoir,*
>   *Il parviendra au chef de son empire;*
> *Vingt mois tiendra le regne à grand pouvoir,*
>   *Tiran, cruel en delaissant un pire.*
> VIII:65

The old man frustrated in his main hope
  Will become head of his empire;
Twenty months will he hold the empire with great power,
  Tyrant, cruel the one following even worse.

Pétain will rule France despotically for 20 months, to be followed by one even worse, Pierre Laval.

Marshal Pétain will be mocked in his efforts to save the slave labourers.

> *Le vieux mocqué et privé de sa place*
>   *Par l'estranger qui le subornera;*
> *Mains de son filz mangees devant sa face,*
>   *Le frere à Chartres, Orl., Rouen trahira.*
> IV:61

The old man mocked and deprived of his place
  By the stranger who will subordinate him,
The hands of his sons will be eaten before his face
  The brethren of Chartres, Orleans and Rouen will be betrayed.

This quatrain foretells Petain's hopeless position. 'The hands eaten before his face' were the slave labourers taken away by the Germans to built fortress Europe. The 'brothers betrayed' were the partisans betrayed by the French informers.

With his tongue in his cheek, Petain will plead to save his slave
labourers.

> Le vielle tribun au point de la trehemide
>   Sera pressee captif ne deslivrer;
> Le veuil non veuil ne mal parlant timide
>   Par legitime à ses amis livrer.
>
> X:85

The old tribune at the point of extreme fright
  Will be pressed not to give up the captive.
The old, not so old speaking timidly of the evil
  To free his friends in a legal way.

Here we have Pétain from a position of weakness negotiating for the
return of prisoners-of-war from a slave labour camp.

Blockaded Great Britain shall make efforts to evade a famine
similar to that of Europe.

> Ceux dans les Isles de long temps assiegez,
>   Prendront vigour force contre ennemis;
> Ceux par dehors morts de faim profligez,
>   En plus grand faim que jamais seront mis.
>
> III:71

Those in the Isles a long time besieged
  Will use vigorous force against their enemies;
Those outside shall die of hunger, being overcome
  By such a famine as never before seen.

Although Great Britain was herd pressed by the submarine blockade,
by the efforts of her navy and the early system of rationing
introduced, the British fared better than their counterparts in
Europe, where many died of starvation.

Children in British cities evacuated and farms will go back into cultivation.

Dedans les Isles les infans transportez,
  Les deux de sept seront en desespoir,
Ceux terrouer en seront supportez,
  Nom pelle prins des ligues fuy l'espoir.
                                    VIII:64

In the Isles the children will be transported
  Two out of the seven will be in despair;
Those of the land will be sustained by it,
  The spade's name taken, the league's hope fails.

The youngest children in southern England were evacuated to safer areas elsewhere, so families were split up. Idle land was made to produce, as noted in the third line. 'The league' was the Axis powers.

The Germans conscripted labour to build 'Fortress Europe': people fled.

De tout Marseille des habitants changee,
  Course et pour suitte jusques pres de Lyon,
Narbon, Tholoze par Bordeaux outragee,
  Tuez captifs presque d'un million.
                                    I:72

In the whole of Marseilles the inhabitants will change
  Fleeing and pursued as far as Lyons,
Narbonne, Toulouse by Bordeaux outraged;
  Killed and captured nearly a million.

France was divided into German and Vichy-ruled territories. This verse tells how the population was fleeing into non-German Vichy. The last line tallies of civilian casualties matches official figures.

General Franco will meet the Axis powers and deny them the Straits of Gibraltar.

De Castel Franco sortira l'assemblee
 L'ambassadeur non plaisant fera scisme;
Ceux Ribiere seront en la meslee
 Et au grand goulphre desnier ont l'entree.

IX:16

Out of Castille, Franco will bring out the assembly
 The ambassador, not complaisant, will make a schism
Those of Riviera shall be in the mêlée
 And to the great one, deny entry to the great gulf.

A most interesting quatrain wherein Franco is predicted by name. After the fall of France the Axis powers and a Spanish ambassador met in Nice to discuss the closing of the Straits of Gibraltar, but Spain would not agree; one of the most important decisions of the war.

Great Britain joins with the Central European nations.

La gent de Dace, d'Angleterre et Polonne
 Et de Bohesme feront nouvelle ligue;
Pour passer outre d'Hercules la colonne
 Barsins, Tyrens dresser cruelle brique.

V:51

The peoples of Romania, England and Poland
 And of Bohemia will form a new league.
To pass beyond the Straits of Gibraltar
 The Spanish and Italians will make a cruel plot.

This is a true survey of conditions in 1938, when the nations of Europe aligned themselves against one another. But once the Sudetenland was given to Germany under the Munich Pact, the rest of Czechoslovakia, 'Bohemia', fell to the Nazis within months.

Romania had no choice but to side with Hitler. The last two lines refer to the fact that Italy had a lot more submarines than Germany, so that when Italy entered the war in June 1940, the submarine blockade of Great Britain could be greatly stepped up. The first two lines may refer to the escaped members of those nations who set up governments-in-exile and fought on the side of the Allies.

King Victor Emmanuel III at last gets his desire when he dismisses Mussilini.

> *Roi trouvera ce qu'il desiroit tant*
> > *Quand le Prelat sera reprins à tort.*
> *Responce au Duc le rendra mal content,*
> > *Qui dans Milan mettra plusieurs à mort.*
> > > VI:31

> The king will find what he desires so much
> > When the Prelate shall be taken wrongly.
> The reply to the Duce will make him unhappy;
> > Who in Milan will put several to death.

The King of Italy had his 'desire' when he was able to dismiss the 'Duce' (Mussolini) and appoint Marshal Badoglio as his Prime Minister. 'The Prelate' was Pope Pius XII, who was a neutral during the War and was widely censured for his inaction. Mussolini had his son-in-law, Count Ciano, executed with others at Milan.

'Operation Dragoon' launched in southern France by the Free French Forces.

> *Classe Gauloise par appuy de grande garde.*
> > *Du grand Neptune et ses tridens souldats;*
> *Rongée Provence pour soustenir grand bande,*
> > *Plus Mars Narbon, par javelots et dards.*
> > > II:59

The French fleet with help of the great guards,
　　Of great Neptune and his trident soldiers,
Shall gnaw Provence by sustaining a great gang;
　　With Mars by javelins and shells.

After the 'Overlord' attack was launched on the French coast on 6
June 1944, another attack called 'Operation Dragoon' was launched
on 15 August 1944 on Provence. It was composed of combined
Anglo-French naval and ground forces. Here 'great Neptune' is the
British Royal Navy, and rockets and shells would be the missiles in
the bottom line.

Germany will invade France twice this century.

Le camp plus grand de route mis en fuite,
　　Guaires plus outre ne sera pourchassé;
Ost recamp et legion reduicte,
　　Puis hors de Gaule du tout sera chassé.
　　　　　　　　　　　　　　　　IV:12

The very great army en route put to flight
　　But they shall not be pursued much further
The army will reassemble and the legion reduced
　　Then chased out of France completely.

The two German invasions of France this century are here predicted.
In World War One the Germans surrendered on French soil, but in the
last war they retreated back to Germany before surrendering at Berlin.

**General de Gaulle, the unlikely, wins when Admiral Darlan is
assassinated.**

Entre Gaulois dernier honoré,
　　D'homme ennemi sera victorieux;
Force et terroir en mouvement exploré
　　D'un coup de traict quand mourra l'envieux.
　　　　　　　　　　　　　　　　III:100

Among the least honoured by the French
    Shall he the victor of his enemy
Power and lands he moved to explore
    When a shot from a dart kills the envious one.

General Charles de Gaulle was 'the least honoured' one while
the 'envious one' was Admiral Darlan, who was assassinated
as he was about to hand over the French navy to the Germans.

Hitler's final hours in the deep bunker in the Chancellory in Berlin.

Les fortresses des assiegés serrés,
    Par poudre à feu profondés en abisme;
Les prodideurs seront tous vifs serrés
    Onc aux sacristes n'advint si piteux scisme.

IV:40

The fortresses of the besieged being confined
    By powder to fire to a profound abyss
The traitors will be shut up alive!
    Never to sextons so pitiful a schism.

In a sense, Adolf Hitler and Eva Braun and associates were trapped in
Berlin's Chancellory bunker. After the pair committed suicide, 'the
traitors' were those left that surrendered.

**Atom bombs will fall on Hiroshima and Nagasaki. A plea to the
immortal God.**

Aupres des portes et dedans deux cités
    Seront deux fleaux et oncques n'apperceu un tel;
Faim, dedans peste, de fer hors gens boutés,
    Crie secours au grand Dieu immortel.

II:6

Near the ports and within two cities
　　Shall be two scourges, I never saw the like;
Famine, within plague, people thrust out by the sword
　　Crying 'Help' to the immortal God.

Both Nagasaki and Hiroshima are ports and before the atom bombs
fell at the end of a long war, famine and disease would be expected
and the people told where to live by the military (third line).

An atom bomb will create a great wind over Hiroshima.

Le grand cité d'ocean maritime
　　Environnee de marets en crystal
Dans le solstice hyemal et la prime,
　　Sera tempté de vent espouvental.
　　　　　　　　　　IX:48

The great maritime city of the ocean
　In its environment of crystal (glass house)
Between the solstices winter and spring
　　Will be tried by a powerful wind.

Here we have Nostradamus predicting the dropping of an atomic
bomb, which will create a powerful blast. The second line describes a
city surrounded by glass or greenhouses, something unheard of in his
day.

151

Chapter 6

THE RISE AND FALL OF COMMUNISM

The quatrains Nostradamus used to describe both the French and Russian Revolutions could be applied to either one, for the causes and results were identical. The rich have ever got richer and the poor poorer, until a point is reached when the inevitable explosion occurs. Then a demagogue takes over, either a Napoleon or a Hitler. Now new factors have entered the scene, automation and the computer both are allowing more work to be done with less labour, making more and more unemployment rife everywhere. This is creating the stage for the next world war.

The Russian Revolution breaks out. Misery to the women, while holy relics burn.

Des innocens le sang de vefue et vierge.
  Tant de maulx faitz par moyen de grand Roge
Saintz simulacres tremper en ardent cierge
  De frayeur crainte ne verra nul que boge.
                                                VIII:80

The blood of innocents, widow and virgin.
  Many evils done by means of the great Red
Holy images dipped in burning candle-wax

Terrified by fear, no one will be able to move.

1917 saw the Russian Revolution (the Red one) break out with its ensuing bloodshed. The ancient churches and their holy relics will be consumed by flames.

The revolutionaries will parade the streets singing their songs.

De gens esclave chansons, chants et requestes,
   Captifs par Princes et Seigneurs aux prisons;
A l'avenir par idiots sans testes,
   Seront receus par divins oraisons.

I:14

The enslaved people will chant songs and requests
   While princes and lords are captive in prison.
In the future, idiots without heads
   Will be received as divine orations.

This quatrain can be used for either the French or Russian Revolutions for in both similar conditions were prevalent. 'Esclave' can mean either 'Slav' or 'enslaved'.

The Russians will become educated, elect their leader and have huge armies.

La gent esclave par un heur martial,
   Viendra en haut degré tant esleuee;
Changeront prince, naitre un provincial;
   Passer la mer copie aux monts levee.

V:26

The Slav people by a lucky martial time
   Will come to be raised to a high degree;
They will change their prince to one born a provincial
   And cross by sea an army raised in the mountains.

This quatrain foretells the great advance that was made by the Russians after their 1917 Revolution. Stalin, their 'prince', was born in Georgia, 'a provincial'. The continuous arrival of reinforcements from the mountainous eastern regions deprived Hitler of Leningrad, Moscow and Stalingrad. Erica Cheetham saw this verse as applying to the Greek situation in 1922, because in our seer's time Greeks were called 'Slavs'. In 1922, taking advantage of the recently defeated Turkey, they attempted to wrest away the Greek populated cities of Asia Minor, but Kemal Ataturk defeated them by inflicting great losses.

The creed of all things held in common among friends will not be practical.

> *En lieux et temps chair au poisson donra lieu,*
> *La loi commune sere faicte au contraire;*
> *Vieux tiendra fort plus osté du milieu,*
> *Le Panta choina philon, mis fort arriere.*
> IV:32

In time and place, that meat gives way to fish,
 The communistic law will be made contrary
The old will hold fast, then move away
 And all things common among friends put behind.

Here Nostradamus wrote that Communism will be tried and will be found wanting.

Communism in Russia will be the first to fail, then others will follow.

> *La loi Moricque on verra deffaillir*
> *Apres un autre beaucoup plus seductive;*
> *Boristhenes premier viendra faillir,*
> *Par dons et langues une plus attractive.*
> III:95

The Morish law will prove a failure
  For another much more seductive
Boristhenes will come to fail
  For gifts and tongues more attractive.

Sir Thomas More (1478–1538) wrote a book called *Utopia*, describing an ideal socialistic state. 'Boristhenes' is Latin for the Dnieper River, thus standing for the Soviet Union of Russia. In the worldwide cold war with the United States of America, the Soviet Union has collapsed financially and economically and has now accepted aid in both those fields from the Americans in order to recover, the meaning of the last line.

7

THE STAR FROM OUTER SPACE

There have been many prophecies of some large heavenly body striking Planet Earth. Mrs Jean Dixon, a very successful seer, wrote that one will strike one of the big oceans. St John the Divine, in Revelations, the last book of the Bible, wrote that the star 'Wormwood' (Rev. 8:10–11) would destroy one third of mankind, animals, ships and creatures of the sea. The greatest American seer of this century, Edgar Cayce, said that before the turn of the century we should expect a sudden catastrophe greater than any known in historical times.

Aerial photos taken of both the moon and Earth show craters made in prehistoric times by objects from outer space. In June 1908 some object now believed to be an asteroid exploded over Tungusha in Siberia, flattening an area of forest 60 miles across. Fortunately, say the experts, that area was not then inhabited. If it had arrived a minute sooner or later, over some other piece of land, millions of people would have died. Only this year it has been reported that an object the size of a football field exploded in the Indian Ocean, west of Western Australia. So the idea of an object from space striking Earth is not preposterous. The questions are – When? and Where? Nostradamus allotted quatrains in number according to the importance of the subject. That he allotted so many to this subject means it is of importance to our future.

Earthshaking fires from the centre of the Earth will damage a new city.

Ennosigee feu du centre de terre.
  Ferant trembler autour de cité neufue
Deux grands rocher long temps feront la guerre;
Puis Arethuse rougira nouveau fleuve.

I:87

Earthshaking fire from the centre of the Earth
  Shall shake around the new city.
Two great rocks will be at war for a long time
  Then Arethusa will redden a new river.

An interesting quatrain. A star, comet or asteroid could strike the Earth with such force that it could reach the molten core of the Earth, thus causing the continental plates to grate against each other (line three). The Continental tectonic plate theory has only been accepted in the last 50 years; where did Nostradamus get the idea from? 'Ennosigee' means earthshaking and 'Arethusa' was the Goddess of natural springs. The last line is describing a river of molten lava. There are so many cities fitting the title 'new city'. A very likely candidate is Naples (Greek: Neapolis). Just to its south-west and only just above sea level is a mud volcano which could erupt just as Vesuvius did in A.D. 79, when it blew its top after being dormant for hundreds of years. Also this area is on the fault line of the African and European continental plates.

A great star or comet shall be seen to burn for seven days.

La grand estoille par sept jours brulera,
  Nuée fera deux soleils apparoir;
Le gros mastin fera toute nuict hurlera,
  Quand grand pontife changera de terroir.

II:41

The great star shall burn for seven days,
   A cloud will make two suns appear;
The big fat mastiff shall howl all night
   When a great Pope changes his territory.

This quatrain needs little explanation. Perhaps this star or comet will leave a trail in the sky upon which the Sun is reflected.

In the near future, other quatrains predict an invasion of Italy from Africa so that the ruling Pope may have to flee. I cannot interpret the sense of the 'big mastiff'.

Mabus, the astral visitor, will cause widespread destruction and loss of life.

Mabus puis tost, alors mourra viendra,
   De gens et bestes une horrible defaite;
Puis tout à coup la vengeance on verra,
   Sang, main, soif, faim quand courra la comete.
                                                II:62

Mabus shall come, then soon after, die,
   Of people and beasts a horrible destruction.
Then all of a sudden, vengeance will be revealed,
   Blood, hand, thirst, hunger, when the comet shall pass.

Is this 'Mabus' the name of a comet which will leave fumes behind, from which people and animals will die? Many people believe the 1917 Miracle of Fatima in Portugal left behind the germs of the 'flu epidemic, which killed as many as the Great War itself did.

Durant l'estoille chevelue apparente,
   Les trois grans princes seront faits enemis;
Frappés du ciel paix terre tremulante,
   Pau, Timbre undans, serpent sus le bort mis.
                                                II:43

During the hairy star's appearance
  The three princes will be made enemies;
The strike from heaven will make peace on Earth shaky,
  Pau, surging Tiber, serpent cast ashore.

This is a continuation of the previous quatrain. Some object is going to strike the Earth from the sky while three world leaders are at odds. Apparently some evil enemy is going to invade Rome from the Lido, near ancient Ostia.

The aimless NATO fleet of the North Atlantic will be without a port.

Le camp Ascap d'Europe partira,
  S'adjoignant proche de l'isle submergée;
D'ARTON classe phalange pliera,
  Nombril du monde plus grand voix subrogée.
                                                    II:22

The aimless group shall leave Europe
  And join up near the submerged island;
The NATO fleet will fold up its phalange
  The Navel of the World, the very great voice replaced.

This is a hard verse to interpret. If some object from space should hit the Atlantic, huge waves would be formed that would sweep over low-lying land. Any naval fleet would need perhaps another port, in this case in the south Atlantic. 'ARTON' could be an anagram for NATO.

Volcanic fallout poisons the water supply of a new city.

Jardin du monde au pres du cité nefue,
  Dans le chemin des montaignes cavees,
Sera saisi et plongé dans la cuve,
  Beuvant par force eaux soulfre envenimees.
                                                    X:49

160

The garden of the world, near the new city
   In the highway of hollow mountains
Shall be seized and dipped into a tank
   Forcing sulphurous water to be drunk.

'The hollow mountains' is Nostradumus's description of the modern city skyscrapers. The tank in the third line would be the city's reservoir. Some commentators believe the 'new city' is New York, for it is surrounded with a garden-like countryside and has skyscrapers. The American seer Edgar Cayce spoke of New York being destroyed about now, to be rebuilt around about the year A.D. 2100.

Australia and New Zealand give help to the distressed Northern hemisphere.

Pres loing defaut de deux grands luminaires
   Qui surviendra entre l'Avril et Mars
O quel cherté! mais deux grands Debonnaires
   Par terre et mer secourront toutes parts.

                                                III:5

Near the eclipse of the two great luminaries,
   Which will happen between April and March
Oh, what loss, but two bountiful ones
   By land and sea shall succour them on all sides.

As the disaster area is in the North Atlantic those places, as we go further from the centre areas, are less devastated. Countries in the Southern hemisphere are relatively unharmed, so food producing countries will be able to provide much needed supplies such as Argentina, Australia, New Zealand, and South Africa.

In Auckland's *New Zealand Herald* of 1 August 1995 there appeared an article on what is described as a 1600 KM gas ball with a core estimated at five to ten times the size of Halley's Comet. It was discovered by astronomer Mr Hale and his photographer Mr Bopp of the Arizona Desert Flagstaff Observatory and named Hale-Bopp.

161

It is reported that it will approach the Earth's northern hemisphere in approximately two years' time. This time coincides with the Nostradamus prediction of when we should expect to see such a comet. The 1980 visit of Halley's Comet certainly was a 'fizzer'. Maybe this visitor will be more spectacular and awe-inspiring, as a comet of this size should be expected to be.

8

WHY IS THERE SO LITTLE ABOUT ISRAEL IN THE PROPHECIES?

I can only find two quatrains about modern Israel in the prophecies. Why? Nostradamus was a descendant of the Hebrew tribe of Issachar, the traditional soothsayers of Israel. His immediate family had long been settled in Granada, tolerated by the Moors who had obeyed Mohammed's command in the Koran to revere 'the People of the Book'. When the Spaniards under Ferdinand and Isabella took Granada in 1492, they insisted that all must accept Christianity, so many Hebrews migrated to those nations that would accept them. The 'Good King René' of Provence was one such sovereign. As they were always a law-abiding, well-educated and intelligent people, it was Spain's loss and Provence's gain, just as the Holocaust was Germany's loss and for those who accepted the Refugees, their gain.

Another reason for the lack of prophecies about Israel was the power of the Inquisition, which Nostradamus had to be careful not to offend. For if he did so, it was a painful death at the stake. We owe our possession of the 'Centuries' to his powerful patroness, Queen Catherine de'Medici, who gave him every encouragement. In any case, every true Christian knows events are unfolding just as the Scriptures said they would.

In World War Two, I served in the New Zealand 2nd Division, a part of the British 8th Army in Africa. I spent some time in the then

Palestine. It was amazing to see an Arab, hardly-a-blade-of-grass field, separated by a fence from a garden with rows upon rows of citrus orange trees watered by hundreds of sprinklers. The victors of Alamein were amply provisioned with Palestinian fruit and vegetables.

On a return Mediterranean visit to Israel in 1981, I saw that the biblical prophecy of the desert had been fulfilled; of desert having been changed to a garden of Eden. Irrigated by water from the Sea of Tiberias, the River Jordan and springs, Israel is now the food-basket of the Middle East. This fearless energetic people from the four corners of the globe have brought the latest ideas with them to transform this ancient country.

Almost every roof has a solar-power appliance, heating water for free. In my country compulsory military training has been abolished since 1960, but here everyone must be prepared to fight at a moment's notice.

There will be new laws in Syria, Judaea and Palestine, before the next century.

> *Nouvelle loi terre neufue occupera,*
> *Vers la Syrie, Judee et Palestine;*
> *Le grand empire barbare corruer,*
> *Avant que Phoebus son siecle determine.*
>
> III:97

> A new law will occupy a new land
> About Syria, Judaea and Palestine
> The great barbaric empire shall he corrupt
> Before the Sun terminates his century.

Here Nostradamus predicts the Hebrews returning and making a new country of their ancient homeland. Also he foresaw the fall of the Ottoman Empire, which was all-powerful in his day, threatening the possession of the Mediterranean Sea itself. In the last line 'Phoebus' is the Sun and before the year 2000.

While the Christians are disunited, the temple will be desecrated.

Quand des croisez un trouvé de sens trouble,
En lieu du sacre verra un boeuf cornu,
Par vierge porc son lieu lors sera comble,
Par Roi plus ordre ne sera soustenu.

VIII:90

When the Crosses will find their senses troubled.
In the sacred place will be a horned bull,
By a virgin pig his place will be filled,
By the King, order will not be sustained.

I feel that this prediction is some event in the near future. 'The crosses' would mean Christians, who are preoccupied for some reason, while vandals replace a horned bull with a young pig. It could be Jerusalem's Dome of the Rock on the Temple Mount, or it could be some other Christian holy shrine. If it is Jerusalem, the mention of a king is interesting. Just recently, the Israeli Prime Minister has recognised Jordan's King Hussein's rights in the Islamic holy places in Jerusalem. In these times of political unrest it is doubtful if he could maintain law and order.

9

EVENTS OF THE YEARS 1955–95

Up until now we have been dealing with proven prophecies to those unfamiliar with history, whether prophecies or not. However, in this chapter we will deal with predictions which have been proven true to those who take an interest in everyday world affairs.

The 1979 dethroning of the Shah of Iran. The Ayatollah Khomeini takes over.

> *Plui, faim, guerre en Perse non cessée;*
> *La foi trop grand trahira le monarque;*
> *Par la finie, en Gaule commencée,*
> *Secret augure pour à un estre parque.*
>
> I:70

Rain, famine, war will never cease in Iran; (Persia)
  Too much faith will betray the monarch;
That finished; in France commenced.
  A secret sign for one to be sparing.

Note the first word 'rain' is an anagram of Iran, the present name of the country, changed in 1935 from Persia. The late Shah's over-confidence in his power and his ministers led to his downfall. The third line predicted the undermining activities of the late Ayatollah Khomeini in his 17-year exile in France and his triumph on his return. The final line is a reprimand to the Shah. His reforms should have been introduced more discreetly.

The Ayatollah Khomeini's name and fate foretold.

> *Le penultiesme du surnom du prophete,*
> *Prendra Diane pour son jour et repos;*
> *Loing vaguera par frentique teste.*
> *Et delivrant un grand peuple d'impos.*
> II:28

The penultimate of the surname of the Prophet
  Will take Diana for his day and rest.
He will wander far with a frenzied head
  And deliver a great people from impositions.

In Nostradamus's day Mohammed was called Mahomet. By taking the last syllable but one we get HOM, but KHOM in English.

The day devoted to the Roman goddess Diana was Monday. To an active old man like Khomeini, who died on a Monday, it could be said Monday was 'his day and rest'. The last two lines describe his life's work to deliver his people from the reforms imposed upon them by the Shah.

The fierce new ruler of Iran will return the hostages to the USA.

> *Le grand satyre et tigre d'Hyrcanie,*
> *Don presenté à ceux de l'Ocean:*
> *Un chef de classe istra de Carmanie,*
> *Qui prendra terre au Tyrren Phocean.*
> III:90

The great satyr and tiger of Hyrcania
  Shall present a gift to those of the Ocean.

An Admiral of the fleet shall issue out of Carmania
　　Who will land at the Tyrrian Phocea.

The present capital of Iran (Tehran) is situated in the ancient
province of Hyrcania, while 'Carmania' is an Iranian province on
the Persian Gulf. 'Satyre' there means a fierce bearded man
(Khomeini). The 'gift' was the 52 hostages seized from the American
Embassy at the fall of the Shah, and then later returned to the
Americans. 'The Admiral of the fleet' was the royalist Admiral
Habibollah who hijacked a gunboat on its delivery voyage to Iran
off Gibraltar, and was forced to be interned, because of lack of
fuel and provisions, at Marseilles, which was founded by ancient
Tyre.

**A new Iranian ruler will be sustained by an old ailing man
(Khomeini).**

> *Quand ceux du pole Artique unis ensemble,*
> 　*En Orient grand effrayeur et crainte;*
> *Esleu nouveau, soustenu le grand tremble,*
> 　*Rodes, Bisance de sang barbare taincte.*
> 　　　　　　　　　　　　　VI:21

When those of the Arctic Pole are united together
　　In the East there will be fear and dread;
The newly elected will be sustained by the great shaky one.
　　Rhodes, Istanbul shall be tainted by barbarian blood.

The Arctic people was the USSR before they disintegrated into the
present group of nations. The 'newly elected' was Iran's first
president, Bani Sadr, who was aided by the Muslim cleric, the
Ayatollah Khomeini. 'Bisance' was the ancient name for the present
Istanbul. The last line is predicting events that will occur in the near
future when much Muslim blood will be shed when the island of
Rhodes and Istanbul are attacked.

An Oriental will use oil as a weapon against the West.

> L'Oriental sortira de son siege;
>   Passer les monts Appenins voir la Gaule;
> Transpercera le ciel les eaux et neige,
>   En un chacun frappera de sa gaule.
>
>   II:29

The Oriental shall leave his seat,
  Passing over the Appenines to see France
Passing the sky, the water and the snow
  And strike everyone with his rod.

Here our seer anticipated air travel. The 'Oriental' was Iran's first president, Bani Sadr, who on his exile flight in a fighter plane flew over the Mediterranean Sea, the snowy Italian Appenines and Swiss Alps to seek asylum in France. The word for 'rod' in French is 'gaule'. As an anagram, make it 'le gau'. As is permissible, change a letter and make it 'le gas', or petroleum. Now we have the threat, that in the future the East will use petroleum or oil as a weapon against the western nations.

The man from the East will also use his rod in Istanbul.

> Du pont Euxine et la grand Tartarie
>   Un roi sera qui voir la Gaule
> Transpercera Alane et l'Armenie,
>   Et dans Bisance lairra sanglante gaule.
>
>   V:54

From the Black Sea and Great Tartary
  A king shall come to see France
Passing through Alane and Armenia
  And in Istanbul leave his bloody rod.

This verse is a confirmation of II:29, the previous quatrain, where President Bani Sadr flew in a fighter plane over the Mediterranean

Sea to dodge pursuers. In southern Turkey there is city called Alanya. Armenia borders on Iran. The mention of Tartary and Istanbul might mean some event in the future not yet fulfilled. The last line means that when the Muslims of the East capture Istanbul, oil will again be a weapon against the West.

The great Arab will invade Iran, then Turkey and Egypt.

Le prince Arabe, Mars, Sol, Venus, Lyon,
Regne d'Eglise par mer succombera;
Devers la Perse bien pres d'un million,
Bisance, Egypte, ver. serp. invadera.

V:25

The Arab Prince, Mars, Sol, Venus, Leo.
The reign of the Church of the Sea shall succumb;
Towards Iran, very near a million,
Turkey, Egypt, the true serpents will invade.

A commentator, Mr McCann, has dated the first line as 21 August 1987, that is midway during the eight-year Iraq-Iran War, in which there were half a million dead on both sides. 'The Church of the Sea' is Christianity, which I have explained previously, and will decline. 'Bisance' (or Istanbul) stands for Turkey, and the 'True Serpents' stands for President Saddam Hussein and his Iraqis. He is also the 'Arab Prince' in the first line. Nostradamus is seldom so direct as he is in this quatrain. He is usually more devious, but here he says definitely 'Hussein will invade Turkey and Egypt'.

The 1990 invasion and liberation of Kuwait state and city.

L'armee de mer devant la cité viendra
Puis partir sans faire langue allee,
Citoyens grande proie en terre prendra,
Retourner classe, reprendre grand emblee.

X:68

The Army of the Sea will stand (guard) before the city (Kuwait)
   Then depart without firing a shot;
The great prey of the citizens will be taken inland (to
      Baghdad).
   The fleet returns to retake a great robbery.

During the Iran-Iraq War, seeing that Kuwait, being a wealthy but tiny state, could be invaded by either of its powerful neighbours, the American Navy was put under the Kuwait flag and stood guard over Kuwait until the war ended, without having to 'fire a shot'. This is the meaning of the first two lines. When the Iraqi invasion took place 'the great prey of the citizens' were those foreign workers who were taken hostage 'inland' to Baghdad to be used as 'shields' in case of retaliatory bombing. When the American 'fleet returned' it found the city had undergone 'a great robbery'; everything movable had been removed to Iraq.

Iraq was twice raised up and twice cast down in the Gulf War.

   Par deux fois haut, par deux fois mis à bas
      L'Orient aussi l'Occident faiblira;
   Son adversaire apres plusieurs combats,
      Par mer chassé au besoin faillira.
                                             VIII:59

   Twice raised up, twice cast down
      The East will also weaken the West
   Its adversary after several battles
      Chased by sea, he will fail in time of need.

This is a prophecy that the 42-day 1991 'desert storm' would be repeated. President Bush in his last days of office, and aware of President Hussein's threat to world peace if he developed an atomic bomb, made a last fruitless, desperate attempt to topple him.

Saddam Hussein will have no protection by sea or by land.

> *Sa main derriere par Alus sanguinaire*
> *Ne se pourra par la mer guarantir;*
> *Entre deux fleuves craindre main militaire,*
> *Le noir l'ireux le fera repentir.*
>
> VI:33

His last hand by Alus blooded
He will not have by sea a guarantee
Between two rivers he will fear the military hand
The black angry one will be repentant.

'Alus' is an anagram for L'USA or the United States of America. So the sense of the verse means that President Saddam Hussein of Iraq will be unable to protect his forces from the American might by sea because the aircraft-carriers provided air cover by sea and land. The American 'military hand', of might, proved much too strong for him. No wonder he became 'so angry and repentant' that he disobeyed United Nations commands.

The life and death of Saddam Hussein.

> *Avec le noir rapax et sanguinaire,*
> *Issu du peaultre de l'inhumain Neron*
> *Emmi deux fleuves main gauche militaire,*
> *Sera murtri par Joine cheulveron.*
>
> IX:76

By the rapacious and blood-thirsty king
Spring from the couch of the inhuman Nero
Between the two rivers on the military left
He will be murdered by a bald young man.

The word 'noir', besides meaning black or swarthy, can also be an anagram for king. 'Peaultre' is a prostitute's couch. That Saddam Hussein is predicted here is confirmed by his plundering of Kuwait and his gassing of civilians in Iran and his own country, Iraq. His life story is an unsavory one. His peasant father deserted his mother before he was born and his stepfather bullied him as a child to steal chickens and sheep to support the large family. On his way to power, he is reputed to have had opponents murdered in such a way that fellow conspirators dared not betray him, because they were also implicated.

'Cheulveron' or 'Chaulveron' is said by one interpreter to mean a diminitive of 'bald'. Another says it is a tenant of some kind, while a third says that it is a surname, such as Joyne Chaulveron. Yet another possibility is that he is a Hare Krishna devotee who keeps his head bald, as against those in the tropics who use long hair as a protection against the sun.

Colonel Gaddafi of Libya deigns to translate Arabic into French.

Prince Libinique puissant en Occident,
  François d'Arabe viendra tant enflammer,
Scavans aux lettres sera condescendant
  La langue Arabe en François translater.

III:27

The Libyan Prince, powerful in the West.
  The French of Arabic will be very enflamed
He, learned in letters will condescend
  To translate the Arab tongue into French.

This quatrain tells its own story clearly. Libya's oil makes Gaddafi one of the oil sheikhs, therefore 'powerful in the West'.

Great danger in Chernobyl explosion. All must flee or the death rays will kill everyone.

Migres! Migre de Genesve trestous,
  Saturne d'or en fer se changera,

Le contre RAYPOZ exterminera tous,
  Avant l'advent le Ciel signes fera.
                              IX:44

Leave! Leave Geneva everybody,
  Saturn's gold will change into iron,
The contrary RAYPOZ will exterminate all,
  Before it happens, the heavens shall show signs.

A most terrifying prediction. This is the 1986 Chernobyl atomic
reactor disaster in all but name. Its fall-out affected the whole of
northern Europe, from Sweden in the north to Austria in the
south. Thousands of people are still dying from its effects and
soils will be contaminated for centuries to come. Only one quarter
of the plant blew up and experts expect the rest to go any time.
Russia has not the funds to shut it down and necessity says it
must keep going. The 'sign' was probably the flash of the explosion
seen from afar.

**Milk, blood and frogs prepared for Dalmatia. What is the
monster?**

Laict, sang, grenouilles escoudre en Dalmatie;
  Conflict donné, peste pres de Balennes,
Cri sera grand par toute Esclavonie,
  Lors naistra monstre pres et dedans Ravenne.
                              II:32

Milk, blood, frogs will be prepared in Dalmatia
  Conflict given, plague near Balennes.
A great cry shall go up through all Slavonia
  Then a monster will be born near and in Ravenna.

I am not clear of the interpretation of this quatrain but I feel sure it
deals with the present unrest in former Yugoslavia. The 'milk and
blood' could be part of the aid being air-dropped by the UN to the
refugees there. 'Frogs' is a derogatory term for the French, who make

up the largest contingent of the UN force. The 'great cry' throughout all Slavonia is certainly present today. The 'monster' of the last line is difficult to define and perhaps only the future will reveal it. It could possibly be the giant American aircraft carriers from which the UN launch their air strikes to try to restore law and order.

The United States and the Soviet Union will one day be friends.

> *Un jour seront demis les deux grands maistres,*
>   *Leur grand pouvoir se verra augmenté;*
> *La terre neufue sere en ses haults estres,*
>   *Au sanguinarie le nombre racompté.*
>
> II:89

One day will be friends, the two great masters,
  Their great power will be augmented;
The New Land will be at its highest state.
  To the Bloody one their number will be reported.

The 'two friendly masters' are the USA and the former USSR. The 'bloody one' is Iraq's President Saddam Hussein. The last line means his spies are trying to get the military and atomic secrets the other two possess. With the collapse of the Soviet Union, its secrets are now for sale to the highest bidder.

The uneasy friendship between the United States and the Soviets will last 13 years.

> *Les deux unis ne tiendront longuement,*
>   *Et dans treize ans au Barbare Satrappe;*
> *Au deux costez seront tel perdement,*
>   *Qu'un benira le Barque et sa cappe.*
>
> V:78

The unity of the two will not hold long,
  And within thirteen years to the Barbarian Satrap.

On both sides there will be such loss
That one will bless the Papacy and its head.

The uneasy peace between the two will not last beyond 13 years then the 'Barbary Satrap' (Iran) will take control. It would appear that both sides will welcome the intervention of the 'Barque', (the Vatican) and its 'cappe' (head) to mediate. According to St Malachy, the next Pope will be the 'glory of the Olive', the emblem of peace. The 13 years probably started when President Reagan and Mikhail Gorbachev signed an arms limitation agreement in 1987.

When the United Nations rule the world, the peace will last 43 months.

> *La regne à deux laissé, bien peu tiendront,*
> *Trois ans sept mois passés feront la guerre.*
> *Les deux Vestales contre eux rebelleront,*
> *Victor nay en Armorique terre.*
>
> IV:95

The reign left to two, it will last a short time,
    Three years nine months will pass before a war.
The two Vestals will rebel against them,
    The VICTOR born on American soil.

Among the five states that have the veto and so dominate the United Nations are the USA and Russia. 'Vestals' were priestesses, now called 'nuns'. In the present three-sided war in Bosnia, three religions are contending, Croatian Roman Catholics, Greek Orthodox Serbs and Muslims. But Islam does not have 'Vestals' or nuns. So only Christian 'Vestals are rebelling'. The 43 months began when both Croatia and Slovenia declared independence in 1992. Under the auspices of the United Nations, President Clinton and his secretary of state, Mr Christopher, have persuaded the three contending factions to sign a peace treaty at Dayton, Ohio, in the USA. Once again Nostradamus predicted correctly when he wrote the VICTOR would be born on American soil.

Cyprus will be denied Union (ENOSIS) with Greece. King seduced, Queen annoyed.

> *En ce temps là sera frustree Cypres,*
> *De son secours de ceux de mer Egee;*
> *Vieux trucidez, mais par mesles et lyphres*
> *Seduict leur Roy, Royne plus outragée.*
>
> III:89

In the time that Cyprus will be frustrated
   Of its help from those of the Aegean Sea;
The old slain, but by cannons and prayers
   Their King seduced, the Queen more outraged.

In the 1960s and '70s the Greek population of Cyprus agitated for union with Greece (those of the Aegean Sea). Under General Grivas, they fought a guerilla war against Great Britain, who held a United Nations mandate to rule Cyprus. The case went to the United Nations council, which awarded independence under Archbishop Makarios as president. King Constantine II of Greece was deposed in 1967 by a military coup (he was 'seduced' to leave). His consort, Frederika was most upset, 'outraged'.

178

10

THE FUTURE AND THE BATTLE
OF EUROPE

Up until now, Nostradamus in his strange devious ways has predicted the future with few errors. If he has been so accurate in the past, is there any reason why he should not also be right in the future? All modern interpreters of Nostradamus pondering over the unfulfilled quatrains realise that he has predicted an invasion of Europe from the East, but cannot imagine its course of action. In my 1981 book I devised a formula which later events have not caused me to alter.

I can provide a quatrain to support every point in my scenario, of which I will now give an outline.

The Invasion of Europe will take place over 27 years. It started in 1980, when Iraq's President Saddam Hussein invaded Iran, and will end in a Muslim defeat in Iran. The terrorist outrages, and the oil shocks of the '70s are all part of a guerrilla war being waged against the West prior to going onto direct open warfare in the future. The five nations with the secret of the atomic bomb have been holding it in a Pandora's Box, trying to keep it closed, but the rest of the world has now prised it open. The know-how to make an atom bomb is now no secret.

The 'Cold War' of attrition waged between the United States and the Soviet Union has left both sides exhausted. Meanwhile the 'Bloody One' has exploited his oil revenues to acquire weapons and the atomic bomb secrets at the expense of providing for his own people's welfare.

179

The purchasing power of the Yankee dollar has now dwindled to a third of its former value over the last 25 years. American bases at home and abroad are being closed at an alarming rate. While those huge aircraft-carriers dominate the Persian Gulf and the Mediterranean Sea the 'Bloody One' will be unable to act. Once they return home for lack of funds, all hell will break loose.

The 'Bloody One' will not act alone. His thrashings in the 8-year Iraq-Iran War and the two lightning wars over Kuwait have taught him lessons. He will be allied with Libya, possible at first with North Korea and Iran, who will assume the leadership, being the most populous nation.

The present Yugoslavia Civil War could be the pretext for the Muslim allies invading Turkey and Egypt. Turkey is a member of NATO, so her fellow-members will impulsively rush to her aid, but will be intimidated or repulsed. Nostradamus makes no mention of the United States taking any part in the Battle of Europe, except perhaps in the final stages. She has been having a number of natural disasters at home of late. At present she is having a trade war with Japan, or it may be an isolationist policy that will keep her from taking any part in European wars unless her interests will demand it. China is now complaining that the USA in a number of ways is recognising Taiwan which she says is a province of China.

The Muslims will now consolidate their hold on Turkey with a confiscation of all non-Muslim owned property and owing to there being so much false paper money available, make gold and silver the only legal currency. Once these reforms are completed, further conquests will be undertaken. The Iranians under their leader will assemble a fleet and plunder the Greek Aegean Islands and put ashore at Salonika a force that will capture Macedonia. They will then call on the island of Rhodes to surrender. Rhodes will refuse and will, unexpectedly, severely repulse an assault. The Iranian fleet will then go to Pylos (once called Navarino) in south-western Greece to refit, train, plan and reorganise. About this time a revolt will break out in Morocco, deposing its king, Hassan, and establishing Islamic law. They then send to Pylos for the Iranian leader to take over. He will do so, then secure the Straits of Gibraltar before going on to Spain to take Granada. At Cordoba, he will hold a religious ceremony of thanks before leaving for Genoa in north-eastern Italy to compete the conquest of Italy there. In Spain a Libyan leader (probably Col Gadaffi) will take over and continue the invasion over the Pyrenees into Southern France.

Meanwhile, from Istanbul the Iraqis (probably under Saddam Hussein) will advance, looting all the way up the Danube valley into France and Germany before answering a call to join the main Muslim army in Southern France.

A third Muslim force will cross the Mediterranean Sea, into Sicily and southern Italy to invade the whole of Italy, causing the Pope and the Vatican to flee and be set up in Germany.

The French under their President, Chirac, will set up a defensive line north of the River Durance, 20 miles north of Marseilles. Here both sides will concentrate huge armies. There will be enormous losses on both sides before the victory goes to the French and their allies. The Muslim losses will be crippling and the French, with the aid of Portuguese ships, will quickly recover the territory lost to the Muslims. The final battle will take place on the banks of the Aras River that borders Turkey, Armenia and Iran. Here the Muslim army will be completely destroyed and their leader captured.

To support this synopsis, I will now provide quatrains from Nostradamus's predictions. I may not be completely correct but I believe I am not that far out.

The long awaited will appear in Asia, not Europe.

> *Tant attendu ne reviendra jamais*
> *Dedans l'Europe; en Asie apparoistra;*
> *Un de la ligue eslu du grand Hermes,*
> *Et sur tous rois des orientz croistra.*
> X:75

The long expected shall never return
  In Europe; in Asia he will appear,
One of the league out of the great Hermes,
  And shall grow over all the kings of the East.

181

'The long expected' could be the promised return of Christ. There certainly would be few Christians prepared to expect him to come from Asia. In Greek mythology, Hermes was the messenger and herald of the Gods. He was also the god of riches and good luck. Can we expect a new religious teacher for the world?

The advent of the Antichrist.

L'Antechrist trois bien tost anniehilez,
   Vingt et sept ans sang durera sa guerre;
Les heretiques mortz, captifs, exilez.
   Sang corps humain, eau rougi, gresler terre.
                                                    VIII:77

The Third Antichrist will soon be annihilated;
   Twenty and seven years his bloody war will last.
Heretics dead, captives exiled, water redden,
   Bloody human corpses, Earth shrunken.

Nostradamus wrote of three Antichrists. The first was Napoleon, who depleted the men of his generation, then Hitler who did the same in his time, and now we have the third who will wipe out more than the other two put together. I believe the year 1980, when Iraq invaded Iran started the beginning of the 27 years, for Saddam Hussein has the unsavoury reputation to fill the role of the third Antichrist. Neither Napoleon nor Hitler was known to have killed anyone in cold blood, but Hussein is reputed to have done so. His soldiers have gassed civilians both in Iran and in Iraq. If the 27 years began in 1980, when he first invaded Iran, then his war will continue until 2007. Of course, the verse does not necessarily say he will live until then.

In July 1999 will come the great king of fear. Who is he and where does he come from?

L'an mil neuf cens nonante neuf sept mois,
  Du ciel viendra un grand Roi deffraieur.
Resusciter le grand Roi d'Angolmois,
  Avant apres, Mars regner par bon heur.
                                X:72

In the year 1999 and seven months
  From the sky shall come the great King of fear
To resuscitate the great King of Angolmois.
  Before and after war will reign merrily.

This is the most mysterious, frightening quatrain of all. Down through the centuries it has puzzled the commentators, myself included. Can we associate this aerial king with the spate of flying saucer phenomena the world has experienced since the last war?

Every thinking person now realises mankind will destroy the environment and himself if he is allowed to continue unrestrained his transgressions. The proliferation of the use of the atom, the use of chemical agents on agriculture, is causing disease and mutations; his pollutions on land and sea will eventually result in his extinction.

Many believe that we will begin the millennium anew. Then the Earth will not be the one we know today; its geography will have changed, new lands will have arisen, replacing the old that will have disappeared, so that future explorers will need to discover the world anew. But overall the human race must never forget the tribulations we are about to undergo.

Nostradamus told us he was prophesying until the year 3797. Bishop Usher, in his time, believed the world was created in 4002 B.C. From that time to Christ we get 4,000 years; until now 6,000 years; and with the millennium that will give us 7,000 years. The number seven is the divine number.

The date in this quatrain, July 1999, is the most precise of any date given by Nostradamus. However it is only some four years away from fulfilment. We should then know its meaning. It may not be as dire as it sounds. Some commentators believe 'Angolmois' is an anagram in old French for 'Mongolois', or Mongolia. The last line means 'Mars' or that war will be raging worldwide, while this even is taking place at the present time.

Turkey's Black Sea coast will be invaded by Iran.

Par feu et armes non loing de la mer negro,
Viendra de Perse occuper Trebisonde;
Trembler Pharos, Methelin, Sol alegro,
De sang Arabe d'Adrie couvert onde.

V:27

By fire and arms, not far from the Black Sea
They will come from Iran to occupy Trebizond;
Be afraid Pharos, and Methelin, the Sun will be merry,
Of Arab blood the Adriatic waves will be covered.

'Trebisonde' was a state on the south Black Sea coast, carved out of the Byzantine Empire before it fell to the Turks in 1453. 'Pharos' here stands for Egypt and 'Methelin' is the Aegean Sea island of Lesbos. As Nostradamus was astray in associating the scene of Nelson's Battle of the Nile with the 'Adriatic Sea', so I think that here he means the Aegean Sea. So the meaning of the last two lines is that Egypt and Lesbos should be prepared for an attack by an enemy, and, regardless of loss of life, they will be both attacked.

Turkey will be attacked by three forces by land and sea.

Par les deux testes et trois bras separés,
La cité grande par eaux sera vexee;
Des grands d'entre eux par exile esgarés,
Par teste Perse Bisance fort pressee.

V:86

By two heads and three separate arms
  The great city by the water will be vexed.
Its great ones, on entry will wander in exile
  By an Iranian head, Istanbul will be hard pressed.

By three forces under two leaders, Turkey will be attacked n its
Black Sea coast and its Mediterranean coast. A naval fleet from
Libya's Tripoli will take Istanbul. The rich merchants of Istanbul
will be stripped of their wealth when the city is taken. The
second line means that Istanbul beside the Bosphorous will be
troubled.

Istanbul will be taken by a surprise rear attack.

Au chalme Duc, en arrachant l'esponce
  Voile Arabesque voir, subit descouverte;
Tripolis, Chio, et ceux de Trapesonce,
  Duc prins, Mer Negro et sa cité deserte.
                          VI:55

The rogue Duke while drawing up the contract
  Will see the Arab sail, as a sudden discovery;
Tripoli, Chios and those of Trapesan
  The Duke taken, the Black Sea and the city deserted.

The 'Duke' is Istanbul's military commander, who is drawing up
a peace treaty when suddenly he will see an Arab Fleet from
Libya's Tripoli. The 'Duke' is taken prisoner and Chios and
Trebizond captured. Everyone will flee from Istanbul and the
Black Sea region.

**The new rulers in Istanbul will change their currency to silver and
gold.**

La trompe fausse dissimulant folie,
  Fera Bisance un changement de loix;

185

> *Istra d'Egypt qui veut l'on deslie,*
>   *Edict changeant monnoyes et aloys.*
>   I:40

The false trumpet hiding its folly
  Shall in Istanbul make a change of laws;
Out of Egypt, one will desire the withdrawal
  Of the edict, changing monies and alloys.

The new Muslim rulers are now firmly established in their capital Istanbul (once known as Bisance) and after a fanfare will announce a change of laws to those based on the Koran, and a new currency based on gold and silver. The Egyptians will object because this change will affect the country's tourist trade with the West, its main source of foreign currency.

A proscription throughout Asia will cause panic and chaos among non-Muslims.

> *Par toute Asie grande proscription,*
>   *Mesme en Mysie, Lysie et Pamphylie;*
> *Sang versera par absolution*
>   *D'un jeune noir rempli de felonnies.*
>   III:60

Throughout all Asia there will be a great proscription
  Also in Mysia, Lycia and Pamphyllia;
Blood will flow because of the blessings
  Of a dark young King filled with felonies.

A proscription throughout Asia and Turkey will cause great distress among the merchants of the Middle East. The Koran decrees that everything belongs to Allah, and extreme Muslims believe that only the true believers are entitled to possess that wealth, so to finance this war of conquest the non-Muslims will be stripped of their possessions, reducing them to beggary. The three cities named are in modern Turkey. The Koran also states that all those who die while serving Allah are promised Heaven, with beautiful women after death. Hence the numerous present suicidal terrorist bombings. This is also the meaning of the last two lines, where a young holy man is promising, after death, forgiveness of sins for those who die in battle. 'Noir' can be an anagram for either a 'King', a black or swarthy person, or both.

A great religious debate will take place in Istanbul.

Dieu, le ciel tout le divin verbe à l'onde,
  Porté par rouges sept razes à Bisance
Contre les oingz trois cens de Trebisconde,
  Deux loix mettront, l'horreur, puis credence.

VII:36

God, the Heavens, all the divine words on the wave,
  Carried by the red shaven-heads to Istanbul;
Against the anointed 300 from Trebizond,
  Two laws will be made; horror, then belief.

An unequal debate on religious beliefs will take place in Istanbul. It could be between two Islamic sects. As Cardinals wear red, so it could be between Christianity and Islam. The mention of 'wave' in the first line means it could be broadcast on radio.

Further religious arguments will continue.

La loi du Sol et Venus contendens,
  Appropiant l'esprit de prophetie;
Ne l'un ne l'autre ne seront entendus,
  Par Sol tiendra la loy du grand Messie.

V:53

The law of the Sun and Venus will be in contention,
  In taking the spirit of prophecy;
Neither one or the other shall agree,
  The law of the great Messiah kept by the Sun.

The 'Sun' here may represent Christianity and 'Venus' Islam.

A great Arab invader will plunder the Danube and Rhine valleys before his French defeat.

> *Dans le Danube et du Rhin viendra boire*
> *Le grand Chameau ne s'en repentira;*
> *Trembler du Rosne et plus fort ceux de Loire,*
> *Et pres des Alpes Coq le ruinera.*
>
> V:68

In the Danube and Rhine shall come to drink
The Great Camel, and he shall not repent of it.
Be afraid the Rhone and more so those of the Loire,
And near the Alps, the cock shall ruin him.

The reforms complete in Istanbul, an Arab army (probably commanded by Saddam Hussein) will advance up the Danube valley against little opposition. This army will threaten all those living near the Danube, Rhine, Loire and Rhone rivers, until it is called to join the vast Muslim army in Provence in France, where a great Islamic defeat will take place, the meaning of the last line.

A fleet under an Iranian leader will pillage the Cyclades before a rest in Pylos.

> *Le chef de Perse remplire grande Olchade,*
> *Classe trireme contre Mahometique;*
> *De Parthe et Mede, et pillier les Cyclades;*
> *Repos long temps au grand port Ionique.*
>
> III:64

The chief of Iran shall fill up in southern Spain;
A fleet of warships shall oppose the Moslem people
Of Parthia and Media and then pillage the Cyclades.
Then a long repose in the great Ionic port.

In this quatrain the timing is wrong; the first line should be last. Before the Arab army left Istanbul, the Iranians will have assembled a fleet; some being captured ships, the others sent from Iran through the Suez Canal, and after defeating an opposing fleet (second line) they will proceed to pillage the Greek islands of the Cyclades in the Aegean Sea. Then after their repulsed assault on Rhodes, they will go to the Ionic port of Pylos in south-western Greece for refitting and training of recruits. That completed, they will go to southern Spain (Olchades being a people who once lived there) at the request of rebels who have revolted.

The Rhodians will appeal for help from the west.

Les Rhodiens demanderont secours,
*   Par le neglect de ses hoirs delaissée;*
L'Empire Arabe revalera son cours,
*   Par Hesperies la cause redressée.*

                                    IV:39

The Rhodians will demand help
    Because they are being neglected by their heirs;
The Arab Empire will re-assess its course;
    For the West, it will correct its case.

In the lightning assault on Istanbul, Rhodes will be bypassed, so the island will demand help from the West (Hesperies and the heirs of Greek learning). The Iranian fleet will have had little opposition up until now and will expect the island to surrender quietly when demanded. This volcanic 90 × 30 mile island has survived many sieges in its long history and will once again repulse its enemies.

This will confound both sides in their future plans, the Iranians being reluctant to leave such a stronghold in their rear but its reduction will be costly for so little plunder.

Malta's facilities needed by Rhodes and Istanbul. They go to the highest bidder.

> *Les conseilleurs du premier monopole,*
> *Les conquerants seduits par la Melite;*
> *Rodes, Bisance pour leurs exposant pole,*
> *Terre faudra les poursuivans de suite.*
>
> II:49

The advisers of the first conspiracy
  The conquerors seduced by the Maltese;
Rhodes, Istanbul for exposing their cities
  The ground will fail the users of flight.

This quatrain appears to say that Rhodes and Istanbul will contend for the use of Malta's airfields, at a time when an invasion of Italy is taking place, but it is the Muslims who offer the best price. The last line seems to mean the airfields are too light or too short for the traffic they will be called upon to provide for.

Looting on Malta's coast will be rife as the island is under siege.

> *La pille faite à la coste marine,*
> *La cita nova et parents amenez*
> *Plusieurs de Malte par le fait de Messine,*
> *Estroit serrez seront mal guardonnez.*
>
> IX:61

The sea-coast shall be plundered,
  By newcomers and relatives introduced;
To many of Malta by the deeds of Messina,
  They kept close will be ill rewarded.

Pillaging will be rife around all Mediterranean coastal areas, many local Muslims taking a leading part.

A coup in Morocco. Its King captured and imprisoned.

Au poinct du jour au second chant du coq,
  Ceux de Tunes, Fez et le Bugie;
Par les Arabes, captif le roy Maroq,
  L'an mil six cens et sept, de Liturgie.

VI:54

At daybreak, at the second cock-crow
  Those of Tunis, Fez and of Bougie
By the Arabs, the King of Morocco will be captured.
  In the year 1607 by the Liturgy.

This quatrain and the next describe a future coup that will take place in Morocco. In 1951, France granted the Sultanate its independence. In 1957, under Mohammed V, it became a kingdom. In 1961, his son Hassan II became the present king. With poor resources and not being an oil-exporting state, Morocco needs to trade with Europe to survive, to the dismay of Islamic fundamentalists, hence the coming revolt prompted by neighbouring Muslim terrorists. No interpreter has yet been able to define the date given in the last line.

Massacre in Morocco. Non-Muslims will be slaughtered.

De Fez le regne parviendra à ceux d'Europe,
  Feu leur cité, et lame trenchera;
Le grand d'Asia terre et mer à grand troupe,
  Que bleux, pers, croix, à mort chassera.

VI:80

From Fez, its reign will come to those of Europe
  Their cities will blaze and the blade will slash;
The great one of Asia, by land and sea will bring a great
    troop
  So that the blues and greens will drive the crosses to death.

In this quatrain is the prediction that the Muslims, after dealing with non-Muslims in northern Africa, will cross the Straits of Gibraltar to begin the conquest of Europe. The great one of Asia is the Iranian leader who plundered the Cyclades of the Aegean Sea, and has now been invited to take over the revolutionary forces.

A learned Islamic leader will overcome Granada, then Genoa.

> *De la felice Arabie contrade,*
> *Naistra puissant de loi Mahometique;*
> *Vexer l'Espaigne conquester la Grenade,*
> *Et plus par mer à la gent Ligustique.*
> V:55

In a lucky Arab country
Will be born, a master of Moslem law;
He will alarm Spain by conquering Granada
And by sea the people of Liguria.

This learned Arab will not necessarily come from Arabia. Apparently, after capturing Granada, he will try to convert its inhabitants to Islam. Then he will later leave by sea to complete the conquest of Italy by landing in Genoa. The Ligurians were originally a tribe who lived in this area.

The great Muslim victor will give thanks to Allah in a public ceremony.

> *Le Bizantin faisant oblation,*
> *Apres avoir Cordube à soi reprinse;*
> *Son chemin long repos pamplation,*
> *Mer passant proi par la Colongna prinse.*
> VIII:51

The Bizantine will make an offering
After taking Cordoba to himself again;

His road, long; repose among the grape-vines
    In crossing the sea to Spain, the 'prey' was the Straits of
        Gibraltar.

The 'Bizantin' could be the victor in the last quatrain. When he crossed to Spain, naturally he would take town and Rock of Gibraltar, thus sealing off the Mediterranean Sea to all non-Muslims. With the Suez Canal and the Straits in Muslim hands, the Mediterranean is now a Muslim lake. He has now retaken Cordoba and Granada, which was lost to Islam when Ferdinand and Isabella of Spain took it 500 years previously in 1492. In a public ceremony he will make an offering of gratitude to Allah for being merciful.

The Moslems will take Granada then, by treachery, Cordoba.

Par les contrees du grand fleuve Bethique
    Loin d'Ibere au royaume de Grenade;
Croix repoussees par gens Mahometiques,
    Un de Cordube trahira la contrade.
                                                    III:20

By the lands of the great river Guadalquivir
    Distant of the Ebro in the realm of Granada;
The crosses will be repulsed by the Moslem people,
    One of Cordoba will betray his country.

I will now return to the North African scene.

An East African leader aided by a Libyan fleet will attack Malta, France and Italy.

De l'Orient viendra le coeur Punique
    Facher Hadrie et les hoirs Romulides;
Accompagné de la classe Libyque,
    Temples Melites et proches isles vuides.
                                                    I:9

From the Orient will come the Punic Heart,
    To vex Hadrie and the heirs of Romulus,
Accompanied by the Libyan fleet;
    The Maltese temples and nearby isles will be deserted.

Some reviewers attribute this quatrain to Emperor Haile Selassie in World War Two, but it fits better here. Some African leader, possibly Libyan, will menace Malta and near islands, France(Hadrie) and Italy (Romulus). 'Hadrie' was Nostradamus' pet name for Henry IV of France.

This African will bring great destruction to Italy and Europe.

Un qui des dieux d'Annibal infernaux,
    Fera renaistre, effrayeur des humains;
Onc plus d'horreur ne plus dire journaulx,
    Qu'avint viendra Babel aux Romains.
                                                II:30

One shall cause the infernal gods of Hannibal
    To live again the terrors of mankind
There never was more horror nor worse will say the journals,
    Will happen or come by Babel to the Romans.

The great Carthaginian general Hannibal brought destruction to Italy, before Christ. Here, Nostradamus wrote, another African will bring similar horrors to Italy again. The Tower of Babel was built near Babylon, so perhaps a destroyer may come from this region again.

All of Sicily and Southern Italy will be plundered and made uninhabitable.

Naples, Palerme et toute la Secille,
    Par main barbare sera inhabitee,
Corsicque, Salerne et de Sardeigne l'isle,
    Faim, peste, guerre fin de maux intemptee.
                                                VII:6

194

Naples, Palermo and all of Sicily
  By barbaric hands will be made inhabitable.
Corsica, Salerno, Sardinia and the Isles;
  Famine, plague, war, end of many evils.

Plundering and looting will now extend right up the Italian peninsula.

Depuis Monach, jusque aupres de Sicile,
  Toute la plage demourra desolée;
Il n'y aura fauxbourg, cite, ne ville
  Que par barbares pillé soit et vollée.

                                    II:4

From Monaco and as far as Sicily
  All the shores will be made desolate
There shall not be any suburbs, cities nor towns
  That have not been pillaged or robbed by barbarians

These lost two quatrains describe the coming state of Italy's western coasts from north to south, which will be pillaged and sacked by the invaders.

The pirates will carry off slaves of all ages and sexes.

Triremes pleines tout aage captif.
  Temps bon à mal, le doux pour amertume;
Proie à barbares trop tost seront hastifs,
  Cupid de veoir plaindre au vent la plume.

                                    X:97

Triremes full of captives of all ages,
  Good times for bad, bitter for sweet;
Hastily, too soon, they will be a prey for the barbarians
  Desirous to see the feather complain in the wind.

This is another quatrain of woe. By sea, great numbers will be carried away to be made slaves; some to good masters, others to be ill-treated. Most will be in doubt whether to change their beliefs and in a quandary as to how to please their new masters.

A cardinal, whilst travelling by sea, will be captured by the pirates.

> Par mer, le Rouge sera prins de pirates
>   La paix sera par son moyen troublee;
> L'ire et l'avare commettra par fainct acte
>   Au grand Pontife sera l'armee doublee.
>   V:44

The Red one whilst at sea will be taken by pirates,
  The peace, because of his influence, will be troubled;
His ire and greed will make him commit a false act
  The great Pontiff will be armed double.

This quatrain is self-explanatory. A cardinal (Rouge), while travelling abroad at sea, will be captured and held for ransom. While in captivity he will commit some unworthy act because of his anger and greed that will annoy the peace plans of the Pope (great Pontiff). The Christian nations will rally to the Pope's support, thus he will be armed both politically and spiritually.

Three temporal leaders will prevail on the Vatican to leave Rome.

> Par la puissance des trois rois tempoulz,
>   En autre lieu sera mis le saint siege;
> Où la substance et de l'esprit corporel,
>   Sera remis et receu pour vrai siege.
>   VIII:99

By the influence of the three temporal kings
  In another place will be placed the Holy See;
Where the substance of the corporeal spirit
  Shall be restored and received as the true seat.

Owing to dangers that will threaten the Vatican, three heads of state
will advise the Pope of the day to change the location of the Vatican
to another country (to Germany) for its security.

Rome will be destroyed spiritually but not temporally.

> *O vast Rome ta ruine s'approche,*
>   *Non de tes murs de ton sang et substance;*
> *L'aspre par lettres fera si horrible coche,*
>   *Fer poinctu mis à tous jusques au manche.*
> X:65

Oh vast Rome, thy ruin approaches
  Not of thy walls but of thy blood and substance;
The harsh one in letters will make so horrible a notch
  The sword wounding all right up to the hilt

Rome will be destroyed, not materially, but metaphorically by verbal
and literary assault.

The Iranians will invade Macedonia when a comet will be seen over
France.

> *Flambeau ardent au ciel soir sera veu,*
>   *Pres de la fin et principe du Rosne;*
> *Famine, glaive; tard le secours pourveu,*
>   *La Perse tourne envahir Macedoine.*
> II:96

A flaming torch will be seen in the sky at night
  Near the mouth and source of the Rhône;

Famine, sword; the help given will be too late
The Iranians will turn to invade Macedonia.

Many interpreters predicted, wrongly, that the comet or torch would be Halley's 1986 comet. This area will be part of the battlefield described in verse II:99, so the torch could be huge flares that will light up the scene. There are two ways to attack Macedonia; going west overland from Istanbul, or landing by sea at Salonika, then going north. That they will 'turn' means they will have been engaged elsewhere.

The Albanian cavalry, by using a culvert, will capture Athens in a surprise attack.

Au grand marché qu'on dict des mensongiers
De tout Torrent et champ Athenien;
Seront surprins par les chevaux legiers
Par Albanois; Mars, Leo, Sat, un Versien.

V:91

In the great market called that of the Liars
By the Torrent and the Athenian field,
They will be surprised by the light horsemen
Of the Albanians; Leo, Saturn in Aquarius.

I like that touch of humour in the first line. During the second World War, when I was camped near Athens, I was intrigued by a concrete lined water-course in the distance. Forty years later, when revisiting Athens, and after having read Nostradamus, I made a point of inspecting the 'Torrent'. Suburban expansion has now made it an open sewer crossed by low traffic bridges. There is a 'field' between the 'Torrent' and the restored ancient Agora (market-place) of Athens. Because of the many low bridges, the Albanians will need very small ponies.

198

A neighing horse shall betray Muslim cavalry dressed as shepherds.

> *Sur le combat des grans cheveux legiers,*
> *On criera la grand croissant confond.*
> *De nuict tuer monts, habits de bergiers,*
> *Abismes rouges dans le fossé profond.*
>
> VII:7

During the battle of the light horsemen
    A horse shall cry out confounding the great crescent;
By night, they shall kill sheep and in their skins, dress as
    shepherds.
    Red gulfs in the deep ditch.

An episode dealing with horsemen, probably in Greece's mountainous northern regions. In the previous quatrain we were told they would be Albanians.

'False dust' or fall-out will bring famine and plague to Greece and the Aegean Sea.

> *Dans Cyclades, en Perinthe et Larisse,*
> *Dedans Sparte tout le Pelloponnesse;*
> *Si grand famine, peste par faux connisse,*
> *Neuf mois tiendra et tout le Chevronesse.*
>
> V:90

In the Cyclades, in Corinth and Larissa
    Within Sparta and all the Peloponnese
So great a famine through false dust;
    It will last nine months in all the peninsula.

This sounds very much like the 1986 Chernobyl disaster. I do not know of any nuclear fuel reactors in Greece.

Solar heat in the Mediterranean will half-bake fish in the sea.

Pour la chaleur solaire sur la mer
  De Negrepont les poissons demi cuits;
Les habitans les viendront entamer,
  Quand Rhod, et Gennes leur faudra le biscuit.

II:3

Because of the solar heat upon the sea
  At Ruboea, the fish will be half-baked;
The inhabitants will come to cut them up;
  When Rhodes and Genoa shall want biscuits.

Another quatrain describing abnormal change, either climatic or caused by atomic bomb fall-out. 'Negropont' is the Aegean Sea island of Ruboea. Both Rhodes and Genoa, as we have already learned, will be under a state of siege, in verses IV:38 and V:55.

We will now return to Spain to resume the Muslim conquest of Europe. The man from Libya shall pierce the Pyrenees to make plans at Carcassonne.

Proche del Duero par mer Cyrrene close,
  Viendra percer les grand monts Pyrenées
La main plus courte et sa percee gloze,
  A Carcassonne conduira ses menées.

III:62

Near the Douro close by the sea, the Cyrene
  Will come to pierce the grand Pyrenees mountains
His big hand and his opening notes
  At Carcassonne he will make his plans.

It will be recalled that the great Iranian leader after taking Granada, left Spain to take Italy's Genoa. Today, Cyrenaica is a part of Libya. So a Libyan leader (probably Colonel Gadaffi) and his forces has taken over to conquer Spain and enter France by way of the Pyrenees.

The Libyan leader will capture Spain and also Malta will be captured.

> *Saturne et Mars en Leo. Espagne captifve*
> *Par chef Libyque au conflict attrapé,*
> *Proche de Malte. Heredde prins vive,*
> *Et Romain sceptre sera par Coq frappé.*
> V:14

Saturn and Mars in Leo. Spain captured
By the Libyan leader in a trick battle.
Near Malta a hereditary one will be taken alive
And the Roman sceptre will be struck by the Cock.

I have no zodiacal reading for the first line. Apparently the Libyan leader will use a ruse of some kind that will win him the battle for Spain. Also I have no clues who will be captured alive near Malta. The last line means the Italians will be defeated by the French.

Near the Pyrenees, aliens will rescue their king, who scares an Italian admiral.

> *Autour des monts Pyrenees grans amas*
> *De gent estrange secourir roi nouveau;*
> *Pres de Garonne du grand temple du Mas,*
> *Un Romain chef le craindra dedans l'eau.*
> VI:1

Around the Pyrenees mounts, a great mass
Of foreign people will rescue their new king:
Near the Garonne and the great Temple of Mas.
An Italian Admiral will fear him on the Sea.

The war is now a Jihad (a Holy War) and a motley rabble will cross the Straits of Gibraltar into Spain, looting as they go. They will lack discipline. In one instance they will leave their leader alone unprotected until the mass arrives to rescue him. The conquering leader will go over the Pyrenees, then down the Garonne Valley to Agen, where the old Roman Temple of Mas still exists. When they were at Sea, the Italian admiral was loath to lock horns with the Muslim leader.

Two famous brothers will be driven out of Spain. Warning given of plague in Adge.

Deux grans freres seront chassez d'Espaigne,
  L'aisné vaincu sous les monts Pyrenees;
Rougir mer, Rosne, sang leman d'Alemaigne,
  Narbon, Blyterre, d'Agath contaminees.

IV:94

Two great brothers will be driven out of Spain
  The elder defeated under the Pyrenees mountains;
The sea reddens, Rhône, blood by Lake Geneva from
    Germany,
  Narbonne and Beziers contaminated by Agde.

I have not been able to identify the two brothers; I presume they are Spanish who will be driven out of Spain, the elder being defeated before he reaches the Pyrenees. The victors will probably see action in the places named in line three. The last line predicts the plague that will be introduced by the three ships mentioned in the next verse.

Three small ships shall enter the port of Agde, bringing plague that will carry off a million.

Au port d'Agde trois fustes entreront
  Portant d' infect non foi et pestilence

Passant le pont mil milles embleront
Et le pont rompre à tierce resistance.

VIII:21

Three small ships shall enter the port of Agde
Carrying not the faith, but plague and pestilence
Passing beyond the bridge, a million will die
And at the third attempt the bridge will be broken.

A 'fuste' is a small shallow draught boat. 'Agde' is a river-mouth port between Narbonne and Marseilles, southwestern France. Nostradamus was a Christian, so 'not the faith' means a non-Christian. Apparently when the ships with the plague arrive, a battle for the port will be taking place, the meaning of the last line.

Down through the centuries, gifts of gold and silver plus precious stones donated to the Church for services rendered have accumulated in the crypts of the ancient churches. The news of those who have plundered the Italian churches and have made themselves wealthy thereby is now widespread. Now like the last century's California gold rush, everyone who can is making their way to Provence to share in the anticipated rape of France. So with the packed masses and shortage of food and poor hygiene, no wonder a plague will sweep the area.

A leader of Trojan blood will drive away the Muslims and restore Christianity.

De sang Troyen naistra coeur Germanique,
Qu'il de viendra en si haute puissance;
Hors chassera gent estrange Arabique,
Tournant l'Eglise en pristine pre-eminence.

V:74

Of Trojan blood will be born a German heart,
Who shall come to so exulted a power
That he will chase away the strange Arab people,
Turning the Church to its pristine pre-eminence.

203

Nostradamus wrote in a number of quatrains about the 'Trojans'. Some historians believe that originally they were descended from Jacob's youngest son Benjamin, the ancestor of Israel's first king, Saul. The tribe of Benjamin caused Israel's first division when they were almost exterminated by the other eleven tribes for sexually violating a visiting Levite and his concubine (Judges, 21:6–7 and 15–18). A part of the tribe escaped to Arcadia in the Peloponnese in southern Greece. Later they migrated to Asia Minor and built the city of Troy. When the Greeks destroyed Troy, one of Priam's 50 sons, Francus, escaped and was the founder of a tribe that eventually arrived in a country to which they gave the name 'France' after their ancestor.

After the fall of the Roman Empire, the Franks gave France its first Merovingian king, Merovech. His grandson Clovis was crowned by the Pope as the ruler of Christendom. A family descendent from the Trojans is believed to live in southern France today. From the words 'chased away' it would appear that the Arab force that advanced up the Danube Valley has been driven off. The last line means that the form of Christianity that will be restored will be shorn of all the impurities it has collected down the centuries.

The Holy Empire will come to Germany: Arabs will be driven out.

Le Saint Empire viendra en Germanie,
Ismaelites trouveront lieux ouverts.
Anes vouldront aussi la Carmanie,
Les soustenens de terre tous couverts.
X:31

The Holy Empire will come to Germany.
The Ishmaelites shall find open places,
Asses too, will want to go to Carmania;
Their supporters shall be covered with earth.

Germany will one day be the centre of Christianity. Ishmael was the first son of Abraham by his slave girl Hagar, and the ancestor of the Arabs. 'Carmania' is a Persian Gulf province of Iran.

Nice will be spared because an unknown benefactor will pay a ransom.

> *Le fort Nicene ne sera combatu,*
>   *Vaincu sera par rutilant metal*
> *Son faict sera un long temps debatu,*
>   *Aux citadins estrange espouvantal.*
>   VII:19

The fort of Nice shall not be fought for,
  It shall be defeated by shining metal.
This fact, will be a long time debated,
  To its citizens, it will be a strange dreadful deed.

When Nice will be threatened, some unknown benefactor will arrange to pay a ransom in gold and silver. Who it is will long be debated. Nice, having escaped destruction, will make it the most important port on France's Mediterranean coast in the coming war.

A powerful king will land near Nice amidst piles of dead.

> *Grand Roi viendra prendre port pres de Nisse*
>   *Le grand empire de la mort si enfera.*
> *Aux Antipolles posera son genisse,*
>   *Por mer la pille tout esvanoira.*
>   X:87

The great king will come to land at a port near Nice;
  The great Empire of dead will be as in hell;
In Antibes, he will put his heifer,
  All the pillage taken at sea will vanish.

Now the resistance is becoming stronger, hence the huge casualties in the second line. Some interpreters write 'Antipodes' instead of 'Antibes', which I think is correct here. The meaning of the line is that he is going to set up a base there containing stores. How is the loot in the last line going to vanish? Are the treasure ships being attacked by aircraft, or by submarines that have come through the Straits of Gibraltar?

Marseilles will be captured by land and sea operations.

Piedz et cheval à la seconde veille
  Feront entree vastient tout par la mer,
Dedans la poil entrera de Marseille,
  Pleurs, cris, et sang onc nul temps si amer.
                                                    X:88

By feet and horse at the second watch
  The entry shall be made, laying waste all by sea
Then the Port of Marseilles shall be entered;
  Tears, cries and blood; never a time so bitter.

The mention of both feet and horses means that Marseilles will only be taken after hard fighting and great loss of life. The second watch is between 4 and 6 a.m.

The great invader of Provence shall bivouac, not be billeted in cities.

En lieu libere tendra son pavillon,
  Et ne voudra en citez prendre place;
Aix, Carpens, l'isle volce, mont Cavaillon,
  Par tous ses lieux abolira sa trasse.
                                                    V:76

In an open place he will wish to pitch his tent
  And not wish to take his place in cities
Aix, Carpentras, L'Ile Vaucluse, Montfavet, Cavaillon,
  In all these places he will hide his traces.

All the places named in the third line are in Provence. A huge army will be massing for the coming battle. In such a situation a wise commander will keep his men away from cities and towns to maintain discipline and avoid disease and desertions. Also spies will find it harder to obtain vital information, the meaning of the last line.

France's President Chirac will be the victor of the Battle of Europe.

Au chef du monde le grand Chyren sera,
Plus oultre apres aimé, craint, redoubté
Son bruit et loz les cieux surpassera,
Et de seul titre victeur fort contenté.
VI:70

The great Chirac will be a chief of the World
Above others, later loved, feared, dreaded;
His fame and praise will be above the Heavens,
And of his title of VICTOR he will be very contented.

All interpreters of this quatrain have been looking for someone with the name of Henri or Henry as the nearest anagram for 'Chyren'. In French I or Y are interchangeable. In an anagram, only one letter is allowed to be changed. Here two letters are changed, but then Nostradamus often made his own rules, ignoring the orthodox. Here is such a case. Both Chirac and Chyren are six-letter words, whereas Henri and Henry are only five each. There is a snag! In northern Africa there is one politician whose name of six letters needs only one change to fit the requirements. However, President Chirac has just entered a seven-year term of President and he is in the right place at the right time to exercise the power needed.

The Gaullist French Presidents have dictatorial powers and already Chirac has shown he intends to use them. Against opposition from his own people and the rest of the world, he intends to proceed with nuclear testing in the South Pacific. If this scenario that I have presented to you is correct, then this expertise and knowledge of atomic bombs may just give France that necessary edge to win this dire battle for the West and Christianity and give victory to France and her allies.

France's President Chirac will call for a modern crusade against the East.

> *Comme un griphon viendra le Roi d'Europe*
> *Accompaigné de ceux d'Aquilon;*
> *De rouges et blancz conduira grand troupe*
> *Et iront contre le Roi de Babilon.*
>
> X:86

> As a griffon shall come the King of Europe
> Accompanied by those of the North;
> Of reds and whites he shall lead a great troop
> And go against the King of Babylon.

If President Chirac is to be the ruler of the world, as in the last quatrain, then he will also be the king of Europe. So he has sent out an appeal for a crusade to all Europeans to come to expel all Muslims who have invaded Italy, Spain and now France. 'Those of the North' will be the Nordics of the Scandinavian countries of Norway, Sweden etc; 'the reds' will be the atheists of the former communist countries, and 'the whites' will be the Christians, because the Pope always wears white.

The Battle for Europe will be fought in Provence, between Islam and Christianity.

> *Aux champs herbeux d'Alein et du Veineigne,*
> *Du Mont Lebron proche de la Durance;*
> *Camps de deux parts conflict sera si aigre,*
> *Mesopotamie defaillira en la France.*
>
> III:99

> In the green fields of Alleins and Vernègues,
> Of the Lubéron mountains near the River Durance;
> The armies of both sides will fight very bitterly;
> Mesopotamia will be a failure in France.

Alleins and Vernègues are small towns in Bouches-du-Rhône, southern France. The Lubéron or Léberon mountains are a range above the River Durance, which runs some 20 miles inland and parallel with the coast from the Alps, to where it joins the River Rhône at Avignon. Alleins is a short distance south of the Durance and 20 miles north of Marseilles. The Lubéron mountains lie north of the river, so the French will occupy the high ground above the battlefield.

There is little doubt that the knowledge that this quatrain predicts that the French will win and that their leader will become famous for the victory, will be a great morale booster for the French troops. France is the last European country to retain something of an overseas empire, and just as her colonies helped Great Britain to survive in the last two World Wars, so her colonies and friends will help her defeat Islam on the River Durance.

Her South Pacific Nuclear tests will aid France here, for her enemy will be dependent on stores, loot, weapons and ammunition captured from their defeated foes to sustain their forces in the field. As we have read, Germany will now be able to assist her.

The last war's Maginot and Siegfried lines, with their deep underground bunkers, will be valuable for both defence and as depots for stores. She will also have the northern European ports to receive supplies from the rest of the world, to help her. As the most vital asset, she will probably have command of the air.

The great Chirac will capture Avignon, to the Vatican's annoyance.

Le grand Chyren soi saisir Avignon,
  De Rome lettres en miel plein d'amertume.
Lettre ambassade partir de Chanignon,
Carpentras pris par Duc noir rouge plume.
                                        IX:41

The great Chirac shall seize Avignon;
  From Rome will come honeyed letters full of bitterness

Embassy and letters shall leave for Chanigon,
   Carpentras shall be taken by a black Duke.

Before or after the great battle on the Durance, President Chirac will seize the strategic city of Avignon on the confluence of the Rhône and Durance rivers. Apparently Avignon's Papal Palace, still existing from the Great Schism (1309–77) will be either unnecessarily damaged or violated by the French army in the seizure of the city. This act will cause both sides to exchange bitter letters, with one side trying to calm the issue. The meaning or whereabouts of Chanignon is unknown, but Carpentas is near Avignon to the north-east. It seems that a capable Muslim leader of negro descent will capture Carpentras.

An expedition will leave Marseilles to aid the Hungarians.

Voille simacle port Massiliolique
   Dans Venice port marcher aux Panons;
Partir du goulfre et Sinus Illirique,
   Vast à Sicille, Ligures coups de canons.

IX:28

The United Sails of Port Marseilles
   In the Port of Venice will travel to Hungary;
Having departed from the Gulf (of Lyons) and the bay of
      Illyria
   Devastation in Sicily and Liguria by cannon shots.

A difficult quatrain. The sense I make out is that an expedition will leave from Marseilles near the Gulf of Lyons via Venice for Hungary. On the way they will bombard Genoa (Ligurians) and Sicily, causing great destruction.

A revolt in the Great Muslim's rear will allow Rhodes to go on the offensive.

> *Le grand Arabe marchera bien avant*
> *Trahi sera par les Bisantinois;*
> *L'Antique Rodes lui viendra au devant,*
> *Et plus grand mal par autre Pannonois.*
>
> V:47

The great Arab will march well ahead,
   He will be betrayed by those of Istanbul
Ancient Rhodes will come to meet him
   And, another greater harm by the Hungarians.

The draw-off of troops for the great Battle on the Durance will leave Istanbul poorly defended, enabling a revolt to break out. The 540 square mile Rhodes has been the only Christian fortress to hold out. They will now be able to send forces to take over the revolt in' Istanbul besides becoming an advance base for future Christian operations. Also the build-up of enemy forces in Hungary will, cause the Muslim leader even greater concern in the Muslim retreat to the East.

The French will chase away the Muslims from Istanbul.

> *L'Ogmion grande Bisance approchera,*
> *Chasse sera la barbarique ligue;*
> *Des deux loix l'une l'estinique laschera,*
> *Barbare et Franche en perpetuelle brigue.*
>
> V:80

The Ogmion shall approach great Istanbul
   To expel the Barbarian league;
Of the two laws, the pagan one will yield,
   The Barbarian and freemen in perpetual friction.

'Ogmion' was the French Hercules, but Nostradamus also used it in verse IX:89 for the young Turks or students whose revolt caused King Louis-Phillippe to be deposed. So here I think a corps of young Frenchmen of students will take over from the now depleted French regulars, to complete the take-over of Istanbul. The use of the word 'freemen' would be consistent with that idea.

The victories of the French will destroy African faith in Islam.

La foy Punicque en Orient rompue
   Grand Jud. et Rosne, Loire et Tag. changeront.
Quand du mulet la faim sera repue,
   Classe espargie, sang et corps nageront.

II:60

The Punic faith in the East broken
   Great Jordan and Rhône, Loire and Tagus will be changed
When the mule's hunger will be satisfied,
   The fleet dispersed; blood and corpses swimming.

The French victories will dishearten the 'Punic' or African adherents of Islam and the countries through which flow the four rivers named will change their allegiance or nationality. 'The mule' is a common beast of burden in the Eastern countries, so I cannot know what our seer means. From the last line it appears that Islam has now lost control of the Mediterranean Sea and the West has freedom of movement although, as we will learn later, piracy is rife.

Transported by Portuguese ships, the French will capture Tarsus.

La grand cité de Tharse par Gaulois
   Sera destruite; captifs tous à Turban;
Secours par mer du grand Portugalois,
   Premier d'esté, le jour du sacre Urban.

VI:85

212

The great city of Tarsus will by the French
  Be destroyed. Those in turbans will be captives;
Help by sea from the great Portuguese;
  First day of Summer of the Sacred Urban.

Tarsus is situated on a plain, 12 miles inland. Adana, to the east, is
the largest city of Turkey's province of Cilicia. The port for Tarsus,
Mersin, is a large and important one with a strategic air base which
played an important role in the 1991 Gulf War with Iraq. Three gates
or passes into the interior exist close at hand. They are the Cilician
Gate into Asia Minor; the Syrian Gate or Belian Pass into Syria; and
the Amanic Gate, or Bogtche Pass, into Armenia and Iran. Saint
Urban's Day is 21 June. Tarsus was the birthplace of St Paul of New
Testament fame. He grew up to be a tent maker in the city.

That the Portuguese will be able to provide ships to transport
the French army to Mersin is proof that the West will control the
Mediterranean Sea.

The final battle of the East against the West will be fought in Iran.

Aux champs de Mede, d'Arabe et d'Armenie,
  Deux grands copies trois fois s'assembleront;
Pres du rivage d'Araxes la mesgnie
  Du grand Soliman en terre tomberont.

III:31

On the (battle) fields of Media, Arabia and Armenia
  Two great armies will meet thrice;
Near the banks of the Aras, the establishment
  Of the great Soliman will tumble to Earth.

The 666 mile-long river Araxes, now called Aras, rises near the Black
Sea, then flows east forming the borders between Turkey and
Armenia, then between Armenia and Iran before emptying into the
Caspian Sea. Near its mouth, some of the water is diverted into the
Kara river to the north while the rest flows into the Caspian Sea. A
number of Turkish sultans were named Suliman.

It is interesting to that both Soloman in Hebrew and Saddam in Arabic mean 'wise man'. The quatrain needs little interpretation. The two armies will meet three times before a decision will be achieved, resulting in the defeat of the Soliman. The French army which destroyed Tarsus will no doubt take part.

The vanquished leader of the East will be led in chains before Chirac.

Le grand mené captif d'estrange terre
  D'or enchainé ay Roy CHYREN offert
Qui dans Ausone, Milan perdra le guerre
  Et tout son ost mis à feu et fer.

IV:34

The great leader, led captive from a foreign land
  Chained in gold, will be offered to King Chirac,
He, who in Ausone, Milan will lose the war
  And all his host put to the fire and to the sword.

'King' here is only another name for President. The vanquished leader of the battle on the River Aras will be taken prisoner, and put in chains of gold. President Chirac apparently, like Churchill overseeing events from afar in World War Two, will do the same in this war, the meaning of the first line. 'Ausone' represents Bordeaux, which in turn represents southern France while 'Milan' here represents northern Italy. The captive presented to Chirac is also the one in the last two lines who loses the war.

The able black-bearded leader will have success. Chirac will free many prisoners.

La barbe crespe et noir par engin
  Subjugera la gent cruelle et fiere.
Le grand Chiren ostera du longin,
  Tous les captifs par Seline baniere.

II:79

The curly black bearded man by a machine
   Will subdue a cruel and fierce people.
The grand Chirac shall free from afar
   All the captives taken under the crescent banner.

There appear to be two separate predictions here. I cannot identify
the man in the first two lines but I can recognise President Chirac in
the last two, who from a distance will be able by his victories to free
thousands of prisoners who had been turned into slaves.

The religion of the Name of the Sea versus the sons of the Moon.

Religion du nom des mers viendra
   Contre le secte fils Adaluncatifs
Secte obstinee deploree craindra,
   Des deux blessez par Aleph et Aleph.
                              X:96

The Religion of the name of the Seas will come
   Against the sect, sons of Adaluncatif;
The obstinate and deplorable sect shall fear
   The two wounded by the Aleph and Aleph.

A mysterious quatrain. Christianity is the religion of the name of the
Sea because the Christian European nations produced the first and
the best sailing ships, then the first steam-boats. This enabled them to
colonise most of the rest of the world. Then their missionaries
converted many of the natives to Christianity. No one has yet been
able to decipher the word in the second line. It seems to mean
'Captives of the Moon'. 'Aleph' is the first letter of the Hebrew
alphabet.

A powerful king will overcome the Muslims of Spain.

Dans les Espaignes viendra Roi trespuissant,
   Par mer et terre subjugant au midi

215

Ce mal fera rabaissant le croissant,
  Baisser les aesles a ceux du Vendredi.
                                  X:95

Into Spain will come a very powerful king
  He will subdue the South by land and sea;
This evil will cause the humbling of the Crescent
  And will lower the wings of those of Friday.

This strong king will subdue southern Spain with apparently little bloodshed, only their obedience being required. 'Friday' is the Muslim holy day of the week.

The pacifier of Italy will be the Christian king of the world.

Selyn monarque l'Italie pacifique,
  Regnes unis Roi chrestien du monde;
Mourrant voudra coucher en terre blesique
  Apres pirates avoir chassé de l'onde.
                                  IV:77

Selyn as monarch will make Italy peaceful
  Realms will be united under this World, Christian king.
His dying wish, is to be buried in a woodland (Blois)
  After having chased the pirates from the sea.

There appear to be two different men to whom Nostradamus gave the name Chyren. In four verses he wrote merely 'great Chyren', while in two others 'Chyren Selyn'. But as we have found before, Nostradamus called the 'Victor' of the Battle on the River Durance 'Chief of the World', so I believe the same man Chirac will be the 'monarch of Italy'.

After such a terrible war, it is to be expected that brigands of former ex-soldiers will be roaming the countryside, raping, murdering and looting. On the Mediterranean Sea, pirates will be hiding in every little cove. To exterminate these brigands and pirates will take considerable time, the meaning of the first and last lines.

A reluctant king will decree against a great league. A new currency.

> *Par lors qu'un Roi sera les siens,*
> *Natif de Blois subjugera Ligures.*
> *Mammel, Cordube et les Dalmatiens,*
> *Des sept puis l'ombre a Roi estrennes et lemurs.*
>
> X:44

When a king is chosen against his own
  A native of Blois will subdue the Ligurians
Of Mammel, Cordoba and the Dalmatians.
  The seven then a shadow of royal money and ghosts.

This seems to be the same king as in IV:77, who will wish to be buried at Blois. He will be reluctant for some reason to accept a crown. The league he will subdue could be the EEC or some Islamic organisation. It could be that 'Mammel' is Memel on the Baltic. The diverse states represented by the cities named means a king of continental proportions. I cannot decipher the last line, except that a new currency seems to be involved.

Soon after A.D. 2002, the new crowned king will give the world peace.

> *Mars et le sceptre se trouvera conjoinct,*
> *Dessoubz Cancer calamiteuse guerre;*
> *Un peu apres sera nouveau Roi oingt,*
> *Qui par long temps pacifiere la terre.*
>
> VI:24

Mars and the Sceptre will be found in conjunction
  A calamitous war under Cancer;
A little later a new king will be anointed
  Who for a long time will pacify the Earth.

The Sceptre here stands for Jupiter, giving the astrological reading of 21 June 2002, marking the end of the great religious war and thus heralding a new era of world peace.

The world nears its last era when the dark nations will predominate.

> *Le monde proche du dernier periode,*
> *Saturne encor tard sera de retour;*
> *Translat empire devers nation Brodde,*
> *L'oeil arraché à Narbon par autour.*
>
> III:92

The world is near its final period,
  Saturn will be late again in his return;
The empire will change into a diverse dark nation.
  Narbonne shall have her eye plucked out by a hawk.

'Brodde' in old French is a word meaning dark-brown or black, touched with an element of decadency. So 450 years since this prophecy was written, we can see in the World today that the darker coloured races are evermore becoming more numerous than the white ones.

As the races interbreed, the brown and black colours will eventually predominate.

Eventually all Earth's creatures will be at peace.

> *La fin le loup, le lyon, beuf et l'asne,*
> *Timide dama seront avec mastins,*
> *Plus ne cherra à eux la douce manne,*
> *Plus vigilence et custode aux mastins.*
>
> X:99

At the finish, the wolf, the lion, ox and ass,
  Timid deer shall be with the mastiffs
No more on them shall fall the manna;
  Nor the watching and keeping of mastiffs.

This quatrain echoes the Bible, which says in the Millenium the creatures of the Earth will be at peace with one another.

EPILOGUE

To those readers who have read through this book, I trust you have found it interesting and thought provoking that Nostradamus writing 440 years ago was aware of so many world events that were to happen during that time and also into our future. In a letter to his king, Henry II, he wrote that his predictions would extend to the year 3797. However like most other interpreters I have taken the remaining unfulfilled quatrains as if they were to be proven prophecies within the next 25 years. So it is possible we are all wrong, and that they, the unfulfilled, will stretch over the next 1700 years. However we must realise he lived in the days of the dreadful Inquisition, so he often wrote to placate or mislead it.

We all live in this apparently decaying world where, as the Bible predicted, belief in the existence of God is rapidly declining. The Nostradamus prophecies confirm my belief in God. If a man in his times could predict the coming events over a 440-year span, then I believe the world is working to a plan. If there is a plan, then there must be a planner. If there is a planner, then that planner whether a he or a she is that entity or being we call God. We also live in a world of degrees of good and evil actions or deeds. Those of us who are fortunate to live to an advanced age and who persevere in doing good deeds usually prevail over those who do evil and are ill rewarded. So I say to those who are God-fearing, stick it out to the end, you will have nothing to fear.